I0795714

STUKA

Dive Bombers, Pursuit Bombers, Combat Pilots

Aders-Held

STUKA

DIVE BOMBERS-PURSUIT BOMBERS-COMBAT PILOTS

A PICTORIAL CHRONICLE OF GERMAN
CLOSE-COMBAT AIRCRAFT TO 1945

GEBHARD ADERS WERNER HELD

Schiffer Publishing Ltd

1469 Morstein Road, West Chester, Pennsylvania 19380

Photo credits:

Grosz 7, Nowarra 55, Zazvonil 4, Petrick 21, Kruse 4, Gliss 16, Federal Archives 12, Dölling 1, Lutz 6, Institute of Prussian Culture 2, Dorner 2, State Illustration Office of Berlin 2, Lendzian 13, Heck 15, Lorant 4, Schliephake 17, Schmitt 5, Thiele 3, Creek 29, VFW 2, Erhard 6, Obermaier 5, Kössler 1, Christl 5, Riess 1, Scheffel 7, Barbas 6, Heise 4, Gläser 2, Lächler 1, Seyffardt 9, Weber 6, USAF 2, Obert 2, Pawlas 1, Brieke 14, Danish Air Force 1, Migge 1, Verreycken 2, Böhme 1, all other photos from the authors' archives.

Drawings in the Appendix: Rainer Gliss

Translated by Dr. Edward Force, Central Connecticut State University

Copyright © 1989 by Schiffer Publishing.
Library of Congress Catalog Number: 89-063368.

All rights reserved. No part of this work may be reproduced or used in any forms or by any means—graphic, electronic or mechanical, including photocopying or information storage and retrieval systems—without written permission from the copyright holder.

Printed in the United States of America.
ISBN: 0-88740-216-X

This book originally published under the title, "Stukas, Jagdbombers, Schlachtflieger," Copyright © 1986 by Motorbuch-Verlag, Postfach 1370, 7000 Stuttgart 1. ISBN: 3-87943-707-6.

Published by Schiffer Publishing, Ltd.
1469 Morstein Road
West Chester, Pennsylvania 19380
Please write for a free catalog.
This book may be purchased from the publisher.
Please include $2.00 postage.
Try your bookstore first.

Contents

Foreword

It is scarcely possible to put together a volume of pictures without exposing oneself to much criticism. Think of the reproaches: Glorification of war and destruction, especially a war dominated by a totalitarian regime, glossing over total defeat, providing new subject matter for those who live in the past, look at the pictures and say: "What wonderful airplanes we had! What would have happened if . . . !" The authors know that they are free from these tendencies and the desire to encourage such tendencies. Like other historians, they are prone to be fascinated by certain aspects of history. The authors admit to being "guilty" of giving in to the fascination exuded by weapons and materials of war in all periods, in this case by the historic aircraft, their technology, breathtaking in its day, and also by the "barbaric portrayal of war".

This volume of pictures illustrates a part of German history. The development and operation of the Luftwaffe's close-combat airplanes. No one denies that they were weapons of war, yet they existed, they are history, and that in itself justifies their portrayal in words and pictures.

For their support in obtaining documentary materials and photos, the authors particularly wish to thank: The Federal Archives-Military Archives, Messrs. Blasig, Creek, P. M. Grosz, Heck, Lendzian, Schmitt, Nowarra, Petrick, Scheffel and Schliephake.

Gebhard Aders and Werner Held

The Combat Pilots of World War I

Like almost all branches of military aviation, combat pilots developed from the armed reconnaissance aviators. Completely within the spirit of the cavalry patrols, which along with their main tasks of intelligence and reconnaissance also carried out attacks on weaker enemy units, the observers of the reconnaissance units occasionally attacked the enemy's marching columns and positions with light weapons.

In tactics and technology, the German military aviators were inferior to their French opponents until 1915. A technical advance of 1915 was the introduction of armed two-seater biplanes, the so-called C-Planes. The C-Plane was *the* working airplane of the German forces for the subsequent war years, being used as a short and long-range reconnaissance plane, artillery observer, and finally as an infantry plane. The infantry aviators became an independent unit within the aerial forces in 1916. During the fight for positions around Verdun, the reconnaissance planes, flying at an elevation of 500 meters, were no longer able to distinguish the positions of neither friends nor foes. Chosen crews were given the task of flying lowest-level reconnaissance, marking enemy positions, dropping information, even ammunition and provisions for the army's leading attack forces. Because of the increasing loss of infantry pilots to ground fire and pursuit, they were equipped with so-called protective aircraft. These planes, by flying low, kept the enemy's ground fire low and secured against enemy pursuit-plane attacks. During the winter of 1916-17 three protective units of six aircraft each were established. By April of 1917 there were nine such units, each assigned to one section of a division.

The protective aircraft belonged to the "Light C-Plane" class, CL for short. They were manufactured by the Halberstadt Aircraft and Hannover Wagon firms, and were two-seater biplanes of 700 to 735-kg dry weight. Their 160-HP Mercedes motors gave them a top speed of about 180 kph. Since they were armed with two machine guns, one firing through the propeller's arc and one machine gun on a swiveling mount in the observer's seat, they were able to do aerial battle with single-seat pursuit planes. In addition, they carried what at that time was a considerable load of airdrop ammunition. At first, hand grenades, sometimes bundled into concentric charges, were used. Then came 4.5-kilogram carbonite bombs with an iron staff and strike plate at their head to 1) prevent penetration into the earth and 2) provide maximum splintering effect on the surface. Other airdrop weapons were the Priester mines used by the mine-launchers and the half-kilogram explosive devices known as flying mice, of which four were loaded into ejection tubes. These were very unpopular among the troops, since the highly sensitive igniters could be detonated in the tubes as a result of strong shaking.

During the 1917 British offensive in Flanders, the protective units had the following tasks:

—Barrage flights over certain sectors of the front, to protect the infantry planes against pursuit-plane attacks,

—Reconnaissance in force, especially over approach roads and battery positions, and,

—Keeping down enemy anti-aircraft fire.

From such an assignment their occured on April 24, 1917 the first fighter-plane operation carried out by the Germans: In the Graville sector of the Somme front, two planes of Protective Unit

7 flew to escort an artillery observer. One of the planes was flown by the unit commander, Captain Zohrer, who noticed that a German supply train had come under fire. Zohrer left the protection of the reconnaissance plane to his men and came down firing at the enemy position. On his first pass, furious defensive fire was directed at him, but on his second flight the enemy weapons were silent; the German infantry recognized its own advantage and stormed the enemy position.

Based on Stohrer's report, the supreme army command authorized the accelerated increase of fighter-plane units. Within twelve months, thirty fighter units with six planes each were created. By the end of the war in the autumn of 1918, another eight units had been formed, and when Fighter Units 39 and 40 were created, each unit was ordered upgraded to nine planes. During the defensive fighting on the Somme front in September of 1918, the fighter units had already been united into battle groups in each army, and the formation of a fighter squadron of four units in each army was planned.

The concept showed the right course. Both in the last German offensive in the West, from March to June of 1918, and in the defensive fighting in the late summer and autumn, the fighter planes became a decisive weapon. When attacking, they complemented the artillery fire, kept down the crews of the enemy position, silenced enemy batteries, wiped out depots in the rear, destroyed aircraft on fields near the front, and broke supply lines. In the last defensive fighting it was the fighter planes that, in massive and uninterrupted operations (even at night), prevented a decisive breakthrough in the St. Quentin sector and thus a catastrophe for the German army.

The lighter armed biplanes (CL planes) of the Halberstadt CL II type, belonged to the first generation of infantry aircraft in 1917.

Right: Stick grenades were also dropped by the crews of Fighter Unit 9.

Center: Fighter Unit Group D, Linselles, 1918. The white or black-and-white fuselage stripes were the identifying marks of the low-flying German planes.

Below: A Halberstadt CL II of an unidentified unit.

Halberstadt CL IV of the 3rd Naval Brigade, 1918. The fuselage is painted in purple and brownish-green camouflage colors. Note the glued-on patches in the wings.

Heavily armored, but ponderous and slow: AEG J I in the ocher and green camouflage paint style introduced in 1918.

The Albatros J I had better flying characteristics than the AEG, but those in command refused it because of its lack of armor protection for the motor.

Junkers J I, the best fighter-plane type of 1918: duraluminum construction with free-bearing wings, 5-mm armor under the fuselage, and an armored radiator in the upper wing.

The Junkers J I coming in to land. Here the extraordinary profile strength of the upper wing is clear to see.

By 1918, 189 Junkers J I had reached the troops. The last types had backward-bending exhaust pipes.

The last fighter-plane type made by Junkers, the CL I, did not reach the front, but was used in the Baltic states against the Red Army in 1919. The pictures show aircraft of Volunteer Air Unit 431 in Latvia.

Between the Wars—The Spanish Civil War

As stipulated by the Treaty of Versailles, Germany was banned from possessing an air force, and from developing or building military aircraft. In the years that followed, Germany was forced into the role of spectator, while the victorious powers developed theories of future air warfare, built up strong air fleets and gained practical experience in the areas of technology, training and operations. But as early as 1926 the conditions for German aircraft construction were relaxed, so that the planning of high-performance airplanes could begin. In 1922 the Junkers firm, using their Russian and Swedish branches, had already begun to build airplanes that in no way corresponded to the Versailles limitations, such as the high-performance two-seat K 47 fighter. From 1926 on, German officers, even though in limited numbers, took part in aerial sports. In the same year a secret agreement was made with the USSR, whereby the Reichswehr was allowed to train pilots and test militarily useful airplanes at Lipezk. Also, the Air Traffic Department of the Reich Ministry began to promote the training of pilots, while the Reichswehr considered the future development of an air force, and industry kept a close eye on developments outside Germany.

After Hitler came to power in 1933, the development of the Luftwaffe gained speed, even though it was disguised. When in 1935 the Luftwaffe was officially declared to be the third branch of the Wehrmacht (breaking the Treaty of Versailles), the concept for its expansion was clear. According to the plans of Wever, Chief of the General Staff, a fleet of strategic bombers, corresponding to the theories of Giulio Douhet, was to form the nucleus of the Luftwaffe, along with medium-heavy bombers and, instead of the tactical light bombers built in France and Britain, the dive bomber for direct army support.

This type of plane was actually not a German invention. At first the U.S. Navy promoted it, because only an airplane that could dive almost vertically at its target, had a chance of hitting a movable target, such as a ship, with deadly accuracy. The Japanese navy followed suit and likewise promoted the development of dive bombers. The German aircraft manufacturers Junkers and Heinkel, very interested in export orders, began to develop diving-capable bombers. Junkers tested diving brakes under the wings of the K 47; Heinkel developed the He 50 biplane in hopes of an order from Japan. Both types were tested in Lipezk, and since the troops were so enthusiastic about their potential for air support, the He 51 fighter and the Ar 66 trainer were tested for use as dive bombers.

The old legend that Ernst Udet was the father of the dive bomber must be refuted. Udet entered the Wehrmacht only in January of 1936, by which time the dive-bomber concept had long since been accepted by the militarists as well as technicians. To be sure, Udet's flying performances with American Curtiss BFC-1 planes had made the diving attack very popular and later caused dive-bomber development to be speeded up. Then too, clever propaganda had made Udet and the Ju 87 dive bomber into a single concept. But one must remember that dive-bomber testing had already been going on in Russia. When the disguised Döberitz Flying Group was established in 1933, this group received numerous He 50 planes for the training of dive-bomber pilots. In the same year contracts were given to Fieseler and Henschel to design a dive bomber. The Schwerin Flying Group was established in 1934, and was a pure dive-bomber unit equipped with He 50's, and later became StG 162 in 1935 and later StG 2 "Immelmann." In 1933, Junkers, on their own, designed a dive bomber, the later Ju 87, in the sure expectation that this design, shelved for the time being, would soon be wanted. In 1935 Fi 98's and Hs 123's were tested. The Henschel plane won the contract and went into production in 1936. Udet was called in to judge the two competitors. The much-maligned dive-bomber opponent, Wolfram von Richthofen, Chief of the Development Department on the Technical Office since 1935, was not opposed to the dive bomber in principle, but only fought against the contemporary conception of a slow airplane that could not escape the enemy guns, and which came within range of flak in its vertical plunge toward its target. Richthofen preferred a plane as fast as a fighter, which attacked its target unbraked in a fast, straight incline, as the Me 210 was later to do. In 1935, still under Richthofen's direction, a further dive-bomber competition was prescribed, this time in two classes:

—light dive bombers, single-seat, 250-kg bomb load, also usable as an auxiliary fighter. Only one design, the Ha 137, was entered. This type really would have been suitable for the future and could have been the ancestor of the fighter-bombers that were so successful later, if only a capable powerplant had existed to help the plane achieve impressive performance. But as it was too slow to be an auxiliary fighter, its development was cancelled.

—heavy dive bombers, two-seat, 500-kg bomb load. Arado entered the Ar 81, Junkers the Ju 87 and Heinkel the He 118.

In January of 1936 Udet joined the Luftwaffe as a colonel. Although he did not know the subject as well as an Inspector of Fighter Pilots should, he worked intensively, under Göring's protection, on dive-bomber development. In March the comparison flying began at Rechlin. The Ar 81 biplane had no chance against the Ju 87 and He 118 monoplanes. The He 118 was a very modern design with retractable landing gear, a 500-kg bomb in a fuselage shaft, and was thus 50 kph faster than the Ju 87, which seemed sluggish with rigid landing gear and the bomb under its fuselage. But it was the more highly developed design and, unlike the He 118, could make dives at an 80-degree angle. But this very characteristic, as well as its slowness, led Richthofen to make the decision to halt development of the Ju 87, since he preferred the He 118. On the next day Udet took over the Technical Office, while Richthofen went to Spain as Chief of the General Staff of the Condor Legion. On June 27, 1936 Udet flew the He 118 himself and forgot to adjust the propeller while diving, and it promptly tore loose. Udet was able to bail out in time, but for him the He 118 was dead and the way was open for the Ju 87.

After the I./StG 162, the II./StG 162 and the I./StG 165 were organized in the spring of 1936, and were all equipped with Hs 123 planes. In the spring the first Ju 87 A-1 planes were sent to the troops; 262 planes in all were contracted for.

In 1936 Germany intervened in the Spanish Civil War with the Condor Legion. When the Bf 109 replaced the old He 51 as a pursuit plane, the latter were used as fighters, and with great success. An even more literally "smashing" success was gained by the three Ju 87 A's that were sent to Spain in December of 1937. The dive bombers' unbelievable precision attacks convinced Colonel von Richthofen of the combat potential of the "braked Stukas". It must be noted that the Spanish Nationalist forces, supported by the German and Italian units, possessed absolute air superiority. The crews of the three Ju 87's were constantly changed, so as to give combat experience to as many pilots as possible.

The death of General Wever in June of 1936 changed the Luftwaffe's equipping concept. The strategic long-range bomber was eliminated, the offensive power was based on medium bombers such as the He 111 and Ju 88, and for cooperation with the army, at least four dive-bomber squadrons should be organized, plus one each with the Training Squadron and Battle Squadron 76. According to the prevailing idea of where the threat of war was possible then, three squadrons were allotted to Air Fleets 1 and 2 on the Polish and Czech borders, and one to Air Fleet 3 in southern Germany. The equipping of the Luftwaffe did not keep pace at all with the speed at which Hitler escalated the political situation. During the Sudeten crisis of 1938 there were not yet enough combat-ready dive-bomber units. On the basis of the Spanish experience, five battle groups, called Fliegergruppen, were hastily formed, with an intended strength of 195 planes, and equipped with antiquated types like the Heinkel He 45, He 50. He 51 and Henschel Hs 123. On August 1 there was only one plane ready for service, a month later there were 136.

In 1938 the Ju 87 A was replaced by the Ju 87 B, which thanks to its 430-HP Jumo 211 powerplant could carry a maximum bomb load of 1000 kilograms. Five of these planes saw service in Spain, with resounding success that founded the legendary reputation of the Ju 87. 964 Ju 87 B's were contracted for, of which 467 had been delivered by the end of August; the I./StG 1, I. and II./StG 2, III./StG 51, I./StG 76, II./(Stuka) KG 76, I. and II./StG 77 and IV.(Stuka)/LG 1 were equipped with them. There was also the 4.(Stuka)/186, a unit that was intended to be based on the aircraft carrier "Graf Zeppelin". The Fliegergruppen were generally dissolved, with only one battle group, the II. (Combat)/LG 2, equipped with Hs 123 and a few Bf 109 E-1 planes, remaining in existence. This was the battle strength with which the dive-bomber and fighter arm went into World War II—thus not a single dive-bomber squadron had its full strength of three units. It is interesting to note that after the Ju 87 B ran out, only limited numbers of the Ju 87 R were to be built, a plane that carried auxiliary wing tanks and was meant to be used against naval targets. Its successor was to be the Messerschmitt 210 fighter-destroyer, which was to carry the same bomb load as the Ju 87 but at almost twice the speed. This type would have corresponded exactly to Richthofen's conception. In addition, experiments were already going on with bomb-carrying versions of the Bf 109 and Bf 110. Finally, it must be noted that even before the war, work had begun on the diving-capable Ar 240, and Dornier designed an armored fighter variant of the Do 17, the Z-8 "Geier".

From the K 47 two-seat fighter built in Sweden, there developed the A 48 experimental plane with which dive-bombing tests were carried out in 1931.

The He 50, officially listed as a multipurpose plane, was the Luftwaffe's first dive bomber. Here is an He 50 B with Siemens SAM 322B motor and two-bladed propeller.

In 1939 an He 50 with a catching hook flew in Olmütz—obviously, landings on dummy aircraft-carrier decks were practiced.

The first flights of the second-generation Stuka competitors, Henschel Hs 123 and Fieseler Fi 98, took place in the spring of 1935. Compared to the Hs 123 (above), the Fi 98 (center) looked old-fashioned. In 1936 the Hs 123 A-1 (below) replaced the He 50 in StG 162.

Ernst Udet (second from right) before one of his demonstration flights with the Curtiss Hawk in 1934. Second from left: Gerhard Fieseler.

Two hopeless entrants in the Stuka competition of 1935: The single-seat BV 137 light dive bomber was of no interest to the Air Ministry, as it was too slow for use as an auxiliary pursuit plane.

The Ar 81 V-2, being a biplane, was inferior to the monoplanes from the start.

HEINKEL

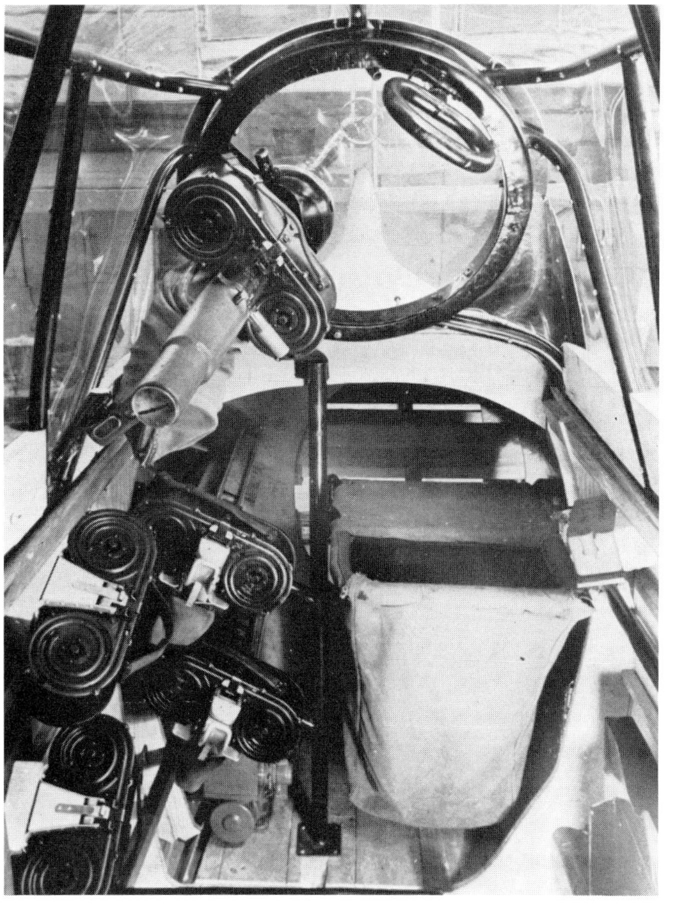

Upper left: Interior view of a Ju 87 cabin mockup. In front of the radioman's seat are the transmitter and receiver of the FuG VII short-wave set.

Upper right: Position B of the mockup, with an MG 15 in a lens mount. The magazines, holding 75 rounds, were emptied in 4.5 seconds.

Right: Instrument panel of the Ju 87 A-1. Visible on the cover from left to right: duct for the windshield ventilation, folded diving visor, rear-view mirror.

In the Stuka competition the slower but better-developed plane, the Ju 87, won out over the technically more progressive He 118.

Left page, above: The Ju 87 D-UKYQ was the third prototype. The plane bore neither camouflage painting nor a national emblem.

Below: He 118 of the A-0 series, identifiable by the covered exhaust cowling.

eft page, above: The
odel for the A-0 series,
e V 4, began flight
esting in the autumn of
936.

elow: In the summer of
937 the Ju 87 began to
eplace the Hs 123 in the
/StG 162. The biplanes
ere turned over to the
ghter units and schools.

his page, above: The
ervice models of the Ju
7 A retained their
egmented paint until
938, the colors being
ark brown 61, green 62
nd light gray 63.

enter: According to
rocedures, the radioman
ad to sit facing forward
order to help the pilot
ith ground-target
bservation.

elow: Only after
npleasant experiences
the air war over
ngland, did the
dioman become chiefly
e air-space-observing
unner.

In the Spanish Civil War, the He 51 planes of the Condor Legion scarcely had a chance as pursuit planes against the Republican I-16 "Rata", but they proved themselves as low-level attack planes.

The success of the Hs 123 as a fighter impressed the "Agrupacion Espanola" so much that in 1938 they obtained more of them and equipped the Grupo 10-G-24 with them.

A Ju 87 A of the Jolanthe Flight with the Condor Legion in 1938.

A propaganda photo from those years: A dive bomber has hit the target in the middle of an intersection. But even with the Ju 87, this was achieved by chance.

In low-level attacks the He 112 the He 112 planes of the Nationalist Grupo 5-G-5, with their 2-cm guns, often destroyed light tanks.

26 **The Ju 87 B was delivered in RLM 70/71 green paint. Only factory-new machines bore the red swastika on the tailfin.**

Details of the Ju 87 B-0 landing gear. From the B-1 series on, the wheel covers were only sprayed dark green.

At the end of 1938, three Ju 87 B-1 planes were in service with K 88 of the Condor Legion. At least one of them bore the Jolanthe symbol on its wheel covers.

Thus did the radioman experience the dive at the target.

Blitzkrieg in Poland, Norway and the West, 1939-1940

For the attack on Poland the Luftwaffe had more than 300 Ju 87 B-1 and 30 Hs 123 planes ready for service. Subordinate to Air Fleet 1 in the north were the I./StG 1, II. and III./StG 2 and the 4.(St)/186. To Air Fleet 4 there belonged the close-combat leader s.b.V., with five dive-bomber groups, the II./LG 2, short-range reconnaissance units, several Do 17 units and destroyers, and meant to fly chiefly for army support with these subordinate groups. The commander was Major General Baron von Richthofen. In the Polish campaign it was already obvious that the Luftwaffe was too weak. The highest priority was given to fighting down enemy aircraft, then came work in cooperation with the army and navy. Ideally, each army would have needed a close-combat air corps under its command. But in the Polish campaign the air forces were far from sufficient, and not even the lone close-combat corps that worked with the 10th Army could always have the use of its dive-bomber groups. Again and again they were taken away from Richthofen and used directly by the Air Fleet to attack airfields. Only the II./LG 2, under Major Spielvogel, flew fighter operations almost endlessly with its poorly armed biplanes, and almost without losses at that. The Hs 123 proved to be easy to maintain and was remarkably able to withstand fire. Thirty of the Ju 87's were lost, and could be replaced immediately from the quartermaster's reserve. The Ju 87 dive bomber proved to be unequaled as a precision bomber against specific targets such as fortifications, buildings, airfields and transportation centers, ands also as a fighter plane. When the Polish Posen Army struck the German 8th Army in the back on September 9, the Ju 87's and Hs 123's were thrown against the Polish attack points in rolling waves. The very sight and sound of the Stukas, plunging down almost vertically with howling propellers, were unnerving for the ground troops. Of course the Ju 87 was theoretically easy to shoot down with anti-aircraft guns, but their tremendously demoralizing effect at first made them as good as invulnerable. Only in later years, when the Stuka terror wore off and the anti-aircraft gunners had gotten used to these planes, did they fall victim to anti-aircraft fire in increasing numbers.

Only the I./StG 1, equipped with long-range Ju 87 R-1 dive bombers, which excelled particularly in attacks on airfields, took part in the attack on Norway.

On May 10, 1940 the attack on The Netherlands, Belgium, Luxembourg and France began. 358 Ju 87 B and R planes took part, plus 40 Hs 123. Some 200 of them were subordinate to the II. Flying Corps; they belonged to the StG 2, III./StG 51 and Carrier Group I./186. Richthofen's VIII. Flying Corps had only the planes of the StG 77, strengthened by the I./StG 76, II./KG 76 and IV./LG 1. As in Poland, the Ju 87's dive-bombed airfields, bridges, railroad intersections, fortifications, prevented counterattacks, silenced artillery and struck troop formations.

The dive-bomber and fighter operations during the crossing of the Meuse in the Sedan area won fame, as also did their strikes against French tank counterattacks at Rethel and Amiens and the attacks on the Citadel of Boulogne. In the fighting at Dunkirk from May 25 to June 4, the dive bombers took their first beating when they were unable to prevent the evacuation of the British expeditionary corps despite some successes. Also, their losses to British fighters were higher than expected.

The concept of smashing enemy air forces and then providing massive army support once they had gained air superiority proved itself again. Dive bombers and fighters paved the way for the capture of fortifications, opened the way for the armored corps, and secured the long flanks of the attack columns against tank attacks. With the brevity of the campaign, the losses were within limits and could be covered from continuing production.

On the eve of the Polish campaign: Fueling, loading ammunition and taking positions on the edge of a war- zone airfield.

At that time one could still get by with this kind of superficial camouflage.

Reconnaissance was often combined with harassing raids. The Hs 126 was able to carry a 50-kilogram bomb for that purpose.

Above: Ju 87 B-1 planes of StG 2 in close-order flight to their target.

Center: Planes of the IV./LG 1 returning. Again and again the commanders had to remind their groups not to split up right after dropping their bombs.

A destroyed wooden bridge in the Polish campaign. The effect of the Stuka bombs on steel and concrete bridges was quite insufficient.

Since the Hs 123 was supposed to be phased out as a combat plane as early as 1939, the planes of the II./LG 2 were not painted with the new 70/71 green camouflage paint.

Several Ju 87 R-1 of the 2./StG 1 carried no bombs under their fuselage during the invasion of Norway, but rather transported crates of tools and ammunition.

Drums for the MG 15 defensive weapon are loaded.

The freight gliders of the air-landed troops can also be counted as close-combat aircraft. The DFS 230 made possible the surprising capture of the fort at Eben Emael.

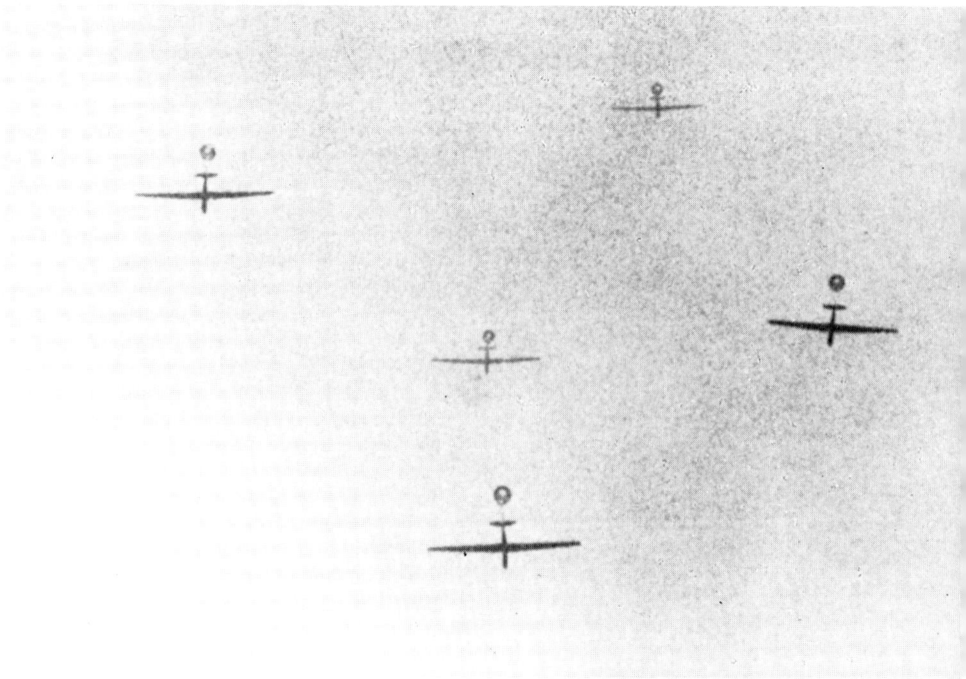

Hanging from their braking parachutes, the gliders plunge toward their target at a 70-degree angle.

Braking skids made landing in the smallest spaces possible.

Lower left: To shoot down ground defenses, these DFS 230's had an MG 15 on the rear fuselage; the MG 34 mounted on the side of the cabin could be fired by the pilot.

Right: A pilot hands the MG 15 to his radioman. On the dark green background, the letters of the unit marking 6G (StG 51) are barely legible.

The 7./StG 51 returning from operations in France, May 1940.

Stukas have smashed the center of a border fort, a tank workshop.

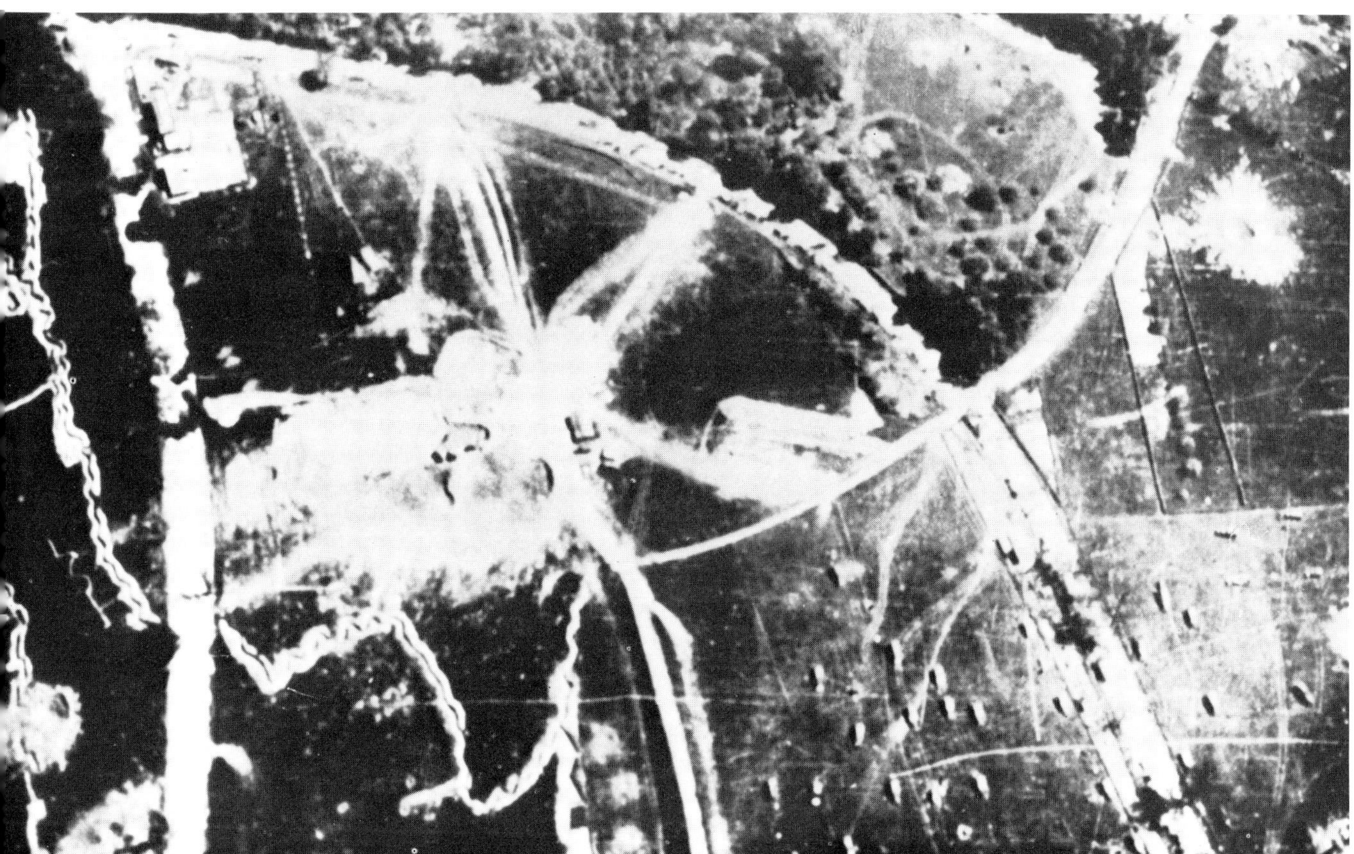

Dive and Pursuit Bombers over England, 1940-1941

After the French campaign, several changes in organization and equipping were made among the close-combat air forces. The planned expansion of StG 51 and 76 did not take place. The III./KG 51 became the II./StG 1, the carrier group I./186 was called the III./StG 2 as of July 9, the I./StG 76 became the first unit of the new StG 3, the II./KG 76 became the III./StG 77. On July 1, 1940 the Testing Unit 210 was established in Cologne-Ostheim out of the 1./ZG 1, 3./StG 77 and 3./186. The purpose was the combat testing of the Bf 109 and 110 as pursuit bombers, plus the learning of new attack procedures. Later the unit was equipped with the Me 210 and became the nucleus of the Me 210 dive-bomber squadron, but at this point in time only three V-models with very inadequate flying characteristics were flying. The Bf 110 D of the 1./EGr 210 were also equipped with 3-centimeter MK 101 cannons for use against sea targets. The II (Battle)/LG 2 was also reequipped. The Hs 123 had done well against infantry and unarmored vehicles, but its two MG 17 machine guns and four 50-kilogram bombs were not enough against larger targets. Since a genuinely new fighter plane was not to be expected before the end of 1940, two units were equipped with Bf 109 E-1/B planes, which might well be described as pursuit bombers, but certainly not as fighter planes.

The contract for the successor to the Hs 123 was competed for by Focke-Wulf with the prototypes of the Fw 189-C series and by Henschel with the Hs 129, both heavily armored twin-engine planes. The Fw 189, with its wingspan of 18.40 meters, was much too big for a fighter and was eliminated, while the Henschel had such a narrow cabin that the pilot barely had a seat, and the power needed to steer it with the short control stick was so great that even the experienced test pilots in Rechlin had a hard time with the plane, which was also very underpowered.

The intensification of the air battle over Britain included dive and pursuit-bomber (EGr 210 and II./LG 2) attacks on Channel shipping and British harbors in June and July of 1940.

On August 13 the large-scale attacks on Britain began, ending in complete failure for the Stukas. The slow Ju 87 tactical plane, which could carry only 450 kilograms and had fully insufficient defensive weapons, was doomed to failure in combat operations. After only a week, the losses of Ju 87's had reached such alarming levels that they had to be withdrawn from the battle. Only in October were they put back in action for night flights over the British Isles and attacks on ship convoys.

The fast Bf 109 E-1/B and Bf 110 C-4, C-7 and D-2 pursuit bombers of the II./LG 2 and EGr 210 set out to succeed the Stukas, but they could not fulfill expectations either. In theory these were the ideal low-level attack planes, fast, strongly armed and capable of carrying 250 kg and more of bombs. But the planes were usually sent into battle in files, rarely in closed units. They were soon met by the RAF pursuit planes and forced to drop their bombs to escape. The situation did not improve after the JG 2, 26, 27 and 53 each set up a pursuit-bomber unit—without the air superiority of the Luftwaffe, the individual pursuit-bomber mission gained no lasting success. In fact, the losses were all the greater. During the autumn of 1940 the Bf 109 E-4/B replaced the E-1; it had an ETC for a 500-kilogram bomb, but it could take off only from paved runways—the much too weak landing gear gave way on grass runways. The pursuit bombers of the Bf 110 C and D series could carry up to two 500-kilogram bombs under the chassis. The Bf 110 E-1 with the more powerful Daimler-Benz 601 N motor was planned from the start as a heavy pursuit bomber with two ETC 50 under its wings. Because of the lack of air superiority over England, the Bf 110 was also taken out of service in September. The last long-range missions were flown by the EGr 210 against Bristol on September 27, 1940; the group commander, Captain Lutz, was lost. From then until March 1941, the EGr 210 flew only surprise attacks on targets near the coast. A good year passed before pursuit-bomber attacks were again flown against Britain and Channel shipping, this time by Bf 109 F-4/B planes of the 10.(Jabo)/JG 62 and 26. But these attacks were nothing but a few pin-pricks, and nothing like the planned harassing actions of the RAF over western France.

Formation flight of the 5./StG 2, summer 1940.

Yellow motor undersides and wing tips were introduced as identifying marks in the air battle over England.

Some "Bertas" had 35-mm Arriflex cameras mounted on their wheel covers to take the impressive film for the weekly newsreels.

A Ju 87 B-1 of the 6./StG 1, with a red and yellow propeller spinner, rolls to a stop.

Since the western campaign, the planes of the 7./StG 51 bore the comet emblem.

Such eye-catching paint jobs were strictly forbidden officially. The shark's mouth could only be painted on for a propaganda photo. II./StG 77, summer 1940.

A "Berta" of the 7./StG 77 ready for action. The bracket for the noisemaking "Jericho siren" was covered with a flat plate here.

Left page, above: The squadron staff units of the StG were equipped with Bf 110 C, which flew ahead of the units on reconnaissance, and could also be used as pursuit protection and low-level attack planes.

Left page, below: In the summer the II./LG 2 had more than forty Hs 123 planes, which had meanwhile been painted 70/71 green. At left is the plane of the commander, Captain Weiss, Notice the double chevrons on the wing and the white stripe along the rear of the fuselage.

A pilot in dress uniform, no radioman aboard, defensive weapons removed: this Ju 87 B-1 of the 9./StG 51 is probably just about to take off on a workshop flight.

The Do 17 Z-6 proved itself as a low-level attack plane in the air war over Britain. Here is an experimental version with a rear periscope and fixed tail gun. The projected fighter version, the Z-8 "Geier", surely would have been successful.

The Ju 88 was also a dive bomber, but was used as such in 1940 only against shipping targets. This Ju 88 A-5 of KG 30 has three coupled 20-mm MG FF in the bow and fixed tail guns, the periscope being for the latter.

In the autumn of 1940 the Stukas flew only missions against Channel shipping or night attacks on targets in England.

A Ju 87 R-1 of the III./StG 1, ready to attack shipping.

A Ju 87 B-1 of the 6.StG 1, its underside painted black to camouflage it at night.

A Ju 87 B-1, with a 500-kilogram under its fuselage, touching down.

Bombs of the Ju 87: SC 10, cast steel SD 50 bombs with organ pipes, and an SC 500 B with three-piece cover.

SC 1000 "Hermann" with heavy-caliber ring tail on a TG 3 transport cradle. The bomb bears the guiding pin belt for use with the Ju 87.

Four SC 10 (explosive bombs, cylindrical, weighing 10 kg) with caps to protect the detonators, and behind them an SC 250 with unusual tail braces.

The movable radiator flaps were a conspicuous identifying mark of the Ju 87 B-2.

Ready for action with the IV./LG 1. Out of the engine cover hangs the activator lever for the flywheel starter.

Ordnance mechanics of the IV./LG 1 installing the detonator of an SD 500 bomb (explosive bomb, thick-walled, 500 kg). France, late summer of 1940.

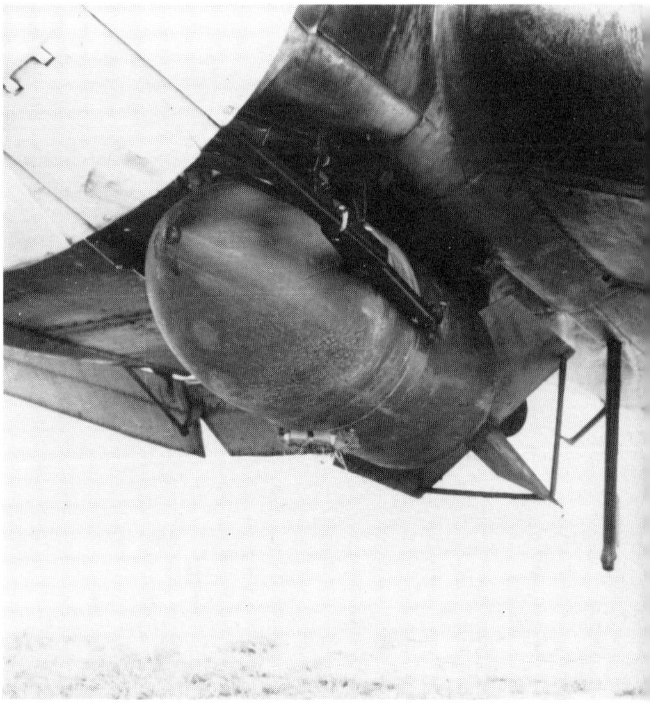

SD 500 bombs under the fuselage of a Ju 87. The length of the fork could be adjusted to fit various bomb calibers.

The red devil on the bomb was the emblem of staff planes of the II./StG 1.

The Ju 87 B's of the short-training unit of StG 1 bore the emblem of the carrier group 186 in its original form: a red eagle with a blue anchor superimposed. The large numerals on the motor and wheel covers were typical of training planes.

After the Stukas returned from the air battle over Britain, more or less intensive training was carried out in France.

Fueling a B-2 of the IV./LG 1.

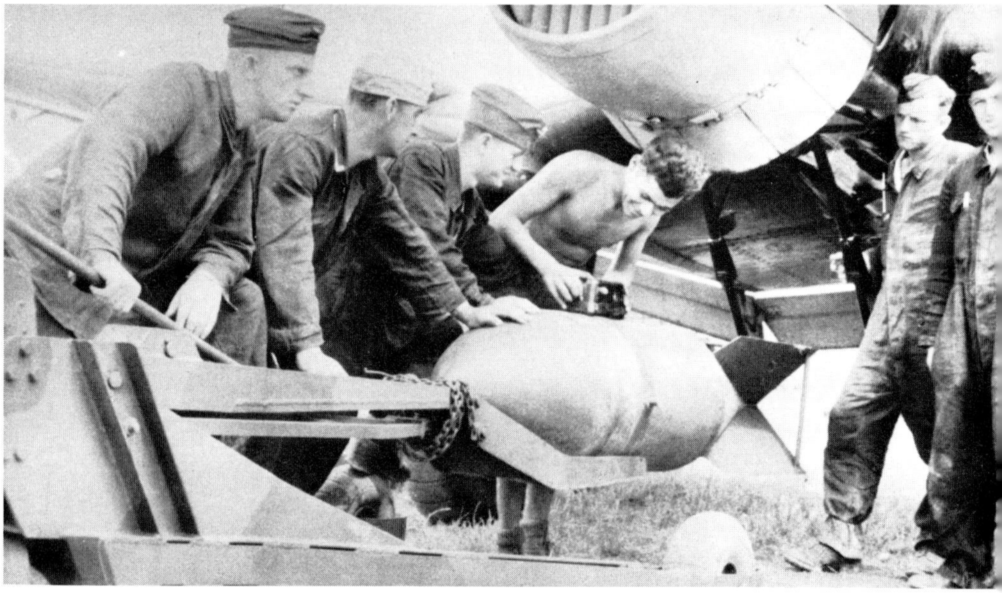

Attaching the detonator switch box to an SD 250.

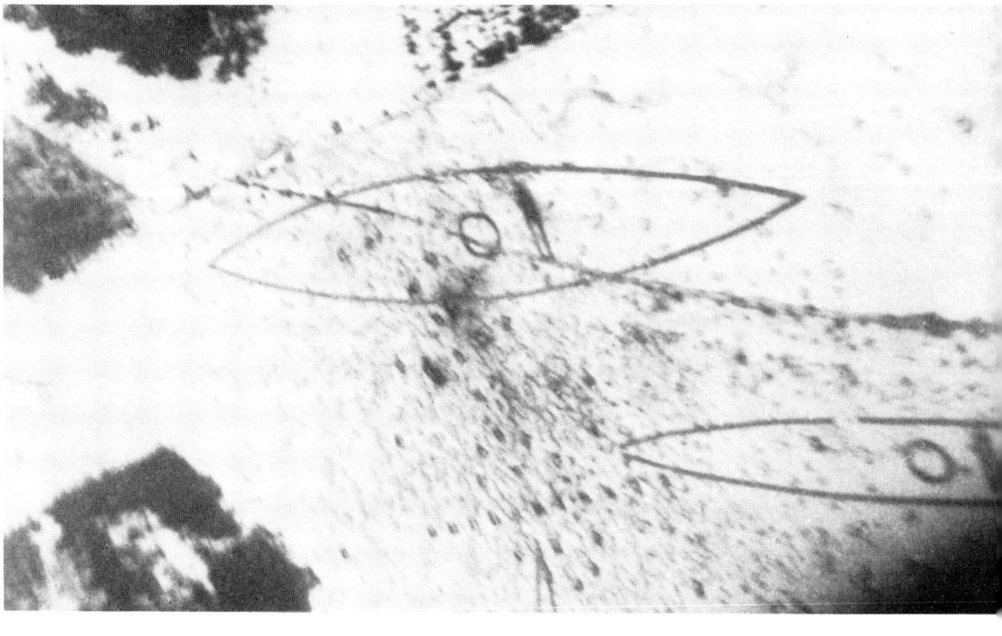

The Stuka school in Graz practiced bombing on the silhouettes of a battleship and a cruiser. The number of misses was considerable!

During the air battle over Britain, pursuit-bomber versions of the Messerschmitt Bf 109 and Bf 110 took on the role of dive bombers. The first experiments had already been made in 1939 with the Bf 109 E-1/B. Here is a plane of LG 2 in 1941.

In 1940 the EGr 210 was equipped with the Bf 109 E-4/B. This one, factory number 1361, carried an SD 250 bomb.

Saddle carriers for four 50-kilogram bombs on a Bf 109 F.

The clamps of the ETC 500 could be adjusted for 250 and 500-kilogram mines.

The 500-kilogram bomb was attached only for a demonstration. In practice the landing gear of the Bf 109 could not hold up under such a burden.

A Bf 109 E-4 of the 10./JG 26 is loaded with an SC 250 bomb.

In 1940 the pursuit squadrons along the English Channel set up pursuit-bomber groups as tenth units.

This SD 500 has a slowing parachute instead of sheet-metal fins, making possible its dropping from very low altitudes.

First Lieutenant Frank Liesendahl's Bf 109 F-4/Bis prepared for a new mission. The yellow stripes on the rear end of the bomb mean that it is filled with explosive type 13. 6./JG 2, Beaumont, March 1941.

Right page, above: This Bf 109 E-4/B of JG 54 bore the symbols of the 7th and 9th units simultaneously.

Below: Some Bf 109 E-4/B planes of the II./LG 2 had RLM 02 gray diagonal stripes on the sides of the fuselage in the autumn of 1940.

Liesendahl's rudder on March 31, 1941.

In the spring of 1941, the EGr 210 was transferred to Vaerlöse, Denmark for refurbishing and provided with the first Bf 110 F-0 planes. Typical of this unit were the yellow fuselage stripe ahead of the cross, yellow leading wing edges and upper wing tips.

Left page: The operations of the EGr 210 proved that the Bf 110 D was a successful pursuit bomber, but that group or column operations without air superiority necessarily led to heavy losses. The plane in the upper picture has the new group emblem.

When no lifting device was at hand, the bombs could also be lifted by hoisting tackle.

The DJ+MN was the model plane for the Bf 110 E-1 series. This pursuit bomber could carry two 50-kilogram bombs under its wings as well as those under its fuselage.

Empty fuselage carriers for two 500-kilogram bombs. Under the fuselage at the rear one can see an auxiliary oil tank.

Above and center: The experiments with special fighter planes begun before the war were carried on in 1940, though scarcely intensified. The Fw 189 V-1b (above) and Fw 189 V-6 (center) were the prototypes for the armored Fw 189 C series. Because of its large dimensions, the model was rejected by the Air Ministry.

The front of an Hs 129 test model's cabin. Note the very small windshield with the thick armor glass and the rough welding seams of the bow armor plates.

Equipped with three 20-kilogram bombs.

Right: A makeshift extra sight on the right landing-gear strut.

The Fi 156 was disguised as a "police stork" plane, but actually intended for use against partisans and U-boats near the coast.

For U-boat hunting, a light French water bomb could be attached under the fuselage.

The Mediterranean Theater of War, 1941-1944

From August 1940 on, the Ju 87 units in France and Germany were replenished and thoroughly trained, especially in operations against naval targets. On the basis of combat experience, the radio equipment had been improved, as was the armor protection for the radioman's seat. In autumn the Ju 87 B-2 reached the troops. The long-range R-2 dive bomber, similar to the B-2, was built in limited numbers. Since the Me 210 was not to be expected in the near future, tests were run with the future Ju 87 D, which had a thoroughly overhauled body and an increase in the motor of 200 HP.

In January of 1941 the dive bombers were sent to a new area: I. and III./StG 2 and the staff of StG 3 were transferred to Trapani, Sicily and were to attack Malta and the Royal Navy from there. Their greatest successes were the damaging of the aircraft carrier "Illustrious" and the sinking of the cruisers "Gloucester" and "Southampton". On Malta itself, the harbor of La Valetta and the airfields were attacked, but the use of rocket-driven armor-penetrating bombs proved to be a mistake—after launching, the bombs swung back and forth before they attained their final flight path. The rocket ignited during the swinging motion and drove the bomb earthward in a straight line, but never in the desired direction. Taking part in the attacks on Malta were, among others, the ZG 26, which made low-level attacks on airfield hangars. In mid-February the I./ and III./StG 1, as well as the III./ZG 26, were transferred to North Africa to support Rommel's Afrika Korps.

In the spring of 1941 the majority of the dive-bomber units gathered on the Russian border. Hitler's decision to "clean up" the Balkan situation by attacking Yugoslavia and Greece first led to the transfer of the close-combat units to Hungary, Romania and Bulgaria. The Balkan campaign began on April 6. The dive-bomber units involved were the I./StG 2, II./StG 2, I./StG 3 and StG 77, plus the II./LG 2 with three units of Bf 109 E-4 and E-7 and one unit of Hs 123 planes. The II./LG 2 was subordinate to the pursuit-bomber unit of JG 27. In all German low-level attack planes, the motor cowlings, control surfaces and wing tips were painted yellow for identification. Of course planes painted so strikingly were hard to camouflage on the airfields, but that was a minor matter to the Axis Powers on account of their air superiority. The purpose of these identifying marks was to prevent losses from anti-aircraft fire by German, Italian and Bulgarian troops. The dive bombers and fighters, the pursuit bombers of JG 77, 27 and LG 2, and the destroyers of ZG 26 once again opened the way for the army, and Athens fell on April 27, 1941. The attack on Crete began barely a month later, and the Ju 87's of StG 2 excelled in driving off the British blockade fleet.

Immediately after this campaign, most of the low-level attack units were prepared for the attack on Russia. The Luftwaffe was able to give only weak support to Rommel's war in North Africa. The III./StG 1, II./StG 2 and I./StG 3 dive-bomber units, united to form StG 3 on January 3, 1942, flew there. The army troops were also supported by the Bf 109 E-7's of the 10./JG 27 and the Bf 110 E's of the III./ZG 26. But these units were weakened by having to continue to attack Malta and the British submarines in the Mediterranean and to protect their own convoys. When large-scale operations like the attack on the fortress of Tobruk were to be made, the dive bombers and destroyers had to interrupt their other assignments—their cover was simply too little.

The dive-bomber missions in North Africa became more and more costly, and not only because of enemy action. The almost impossible servicing conditions in the desert also decreased combat readiness, though special tropic versions were used in North Africa. Difficulties in supplying fuel also helped to keep the dive bombers on the ground. With the collapse of Tunis in May of 1943, the Ju 87 disappeared for a time from the southern theater of war. In November of 1943 the StG 3 was again summoned from the eastern front to support the German landing forces in the taking of the Aegean Islands.

In November of 1942 a completely new type of plane appeared in North Africa, the Hs 129. After unsatisfactory trials with the As 411-powered Hs 129 A, production of the B version, powered by two 700-HP Gnome/Rhône motors, began in November. Equipped with insufficient moist-air filters, the motor often broke down in North Africa, and the Hs 129 B-1 planes of the 4./Sch.G 2 were lost within two months. In February of 1943 an Hs 129 unit, the 8./Sch.G 2, again arrived in North Africa—it had been formed of the pursuit-bomber units of JG 27 and 53. The planes flew fighter missions from Tunis against Allied armored units and were quite successful. With the R 2 armament package, the 30-mm MK 101 gun, the Hs 129 was an excellent antitank plane, and in R 4 form it had six MG 17 and two MG 151 machine guns. When it was clear that Tunis would fall, the expensive planes were transferred via Sicily to the eastern front. The Sch.G 2 had been established at the end of 1942, its first unit being the former Bf 109-equipped III./ZG 1, now equipped with Fw 190 planes. A strengthened unit, commanded by Captain Dörnbrack, was transferred to North Africa in the spring of 1943.

Since an Allied landing in Sicily was to be expected after their victory in North Africa, the Sch.G 2 was pulled together in Sicily and southern Italy as an anti-invasion squadron, equipped with pursuit-bomber versions of the Fw 190. When the Allies landed on Sicily on June 10, 1943, the Fw 190 units, carrying 500 and 1000-kilogram bombs, were supposed to make mass attacks on the Allied ships, but this never took place. The squadron was broken up into units, as was the already summoned units of SKG 10. What remained of these groups was absorbed into the new SG 4 and 10 on October 10, 1943. Until mid-1944 both SG 4 groups remained in Italy, where they were to be transferred to the invasion front in Normandy and then to the eastern front.

Since the tremendous Allied air superiority in the south turned daily operations into hopeless suicide runs, the Luftwaffe was limited to night flights. The Einhorn (Unicorn) Special Group, a strengthened Fw 190 F-8 group, was in Italy in the autumn of 1944, as was the Night Battle Group 9, equipped with Ju 87 D planes. The Einhorn group was renamed the 13./KG 200 in December of 1944. In the autumn of 1944 as well, additional night-fighting groups were transferred to the Apennine front: the NSGr 2 with three units of Ju 87 D-3 and D-5 planes, plus one unit with Ar 66 and Go 145, then the 1./NSGr 4 with Ju 87 D-8 and the NSGr 6 with Ju 87 D's. The NSGr 7 deserves special mention; it was formed of the Croatian night reconnaissance group and flew night attacks against Yuglsoav partisans with a mixture of Fiat Cr 42, Caproni 314, Macchi MC 220 and Hs 126 planes.

A Ju 87 B of the III./StG 1 approaching Trapani.

A plane of the 1./StG 3 on a workshop flight.

To attack warships and bomb Malta, several of the upgraded dive-bomber groups were transferred to Sicily early in 1941.

Ju 87 R's of the 1./StG 1 head back to Sicily with empty bomb hooks. The white identifying marks of the Italians were used on German planes operating in the Mediterranean area.

Hs 123 of the II./LG 2 in dark green RLM 71 paint, with yellow motor cowling and rudder. As can be seen, fighter planes bore the black triangle and infantry assault emblem even then.

In the Balkan campaign, aircraft identifying marks were more important than camouflage, and thus all low-level attack planes were painted with conspicuous yellow markings.

Ju 87 B of the 2./StG 2, with yellow nose, on a Greek airfield. At the right rear is a captured Blenheim.

Pursuit bombers of the Bf 109 E-4 and E-7 types with the II./LG 2 and JG 27, which worked together during the Balkan campaign. All planes bore numerals on their yellow motor cowlings, though in varying forms.

After the end of the Balkan campaign, the 1./StG 2 was at first transferred to Romania, with the motor cowlings painted green again.

Bf 109 F planes of the I./LG 2, recognizable by their red control surfaces, after successful fighting against ships in the Aegean Sea, April 1941.

In the spring of 1941 the first dive bombers were transferred to North Africa: Ju 87 R-2 of the III./StG 1 in the outskirts of Tripoli. The conditions for servicing the planes were more than primitive.

Left page, above: In the Balkan campaign it was already seen that the too-narrow wheel covers of the Hs 123 quickly bent while rolling on unpaved fields and had to be removed.

Center: Ju 87 R of the I./StG 3 over the Greek coast. The unit then used the S1+identification.

Below: A unit of Ju 87 B-2 planes on a transfer flight over the Mediterranean. In addition to their white bellybands, the planes have white stripes on the edges of their control surfaces.

Above: This unreal photo was taken only at the special request of the photographer! Because of the amount of dust they stirred up, the planes always took off side by side.

Center: Here it can be seen clearly how misplaced the black and green camouflage paint of the Ju 87 B-2 is, compared to the practical desert camouflage of the Macchi MC 200.

Only at the end of 1941 were the B and R versions delivered to the X. Flying Corps in tropic form: the upper paint was yellow-brown 79, the underside blue 78, the air intakes with sand filters had a rectangular cross-section, the MG 17 in the wings had additional sand protection for their muzzles.

Ju 87 R-4 of the I./StG 1 with SD 1000 bomb, probably before a mission against the fortress at Tobruk.

Ju 87 R-4 in action against enemy preparations. Under its wings the plane carries four bundles of five SD 10 bombs each, plus a 250-kilogram bomb under the fuselage.

Ju 87 B-2 of StG 3, with additional armor for the gunner. Because of the white fuselage band, the identification number is far to the rear.

Ju 87 B-2 of the I./StG I in perfect desert camouflage: olive green spots on a sand-tan background. Under its wings the plane carries bundles of five 10-kilogram bombs each, held together by a single protective cap.

Short-range protection of a dive-bomber group that broke up after bombing was a thankless task for the escort fighters. In the Bf 109 E-7 is the group adjutant of the I./JG 27, First Lieutenant Franzisket.

This was a case of shooting cannons at sparrows: Artillery fire and Stuka bombs against a spread-out and staggered British attack group. The sand stirred up by the impacts led to an overestimation of the bombs' effectiveness and prevented seeing the enemy's movements.

Ju 87 B-2 of the 3./StG 3 turning back after dropping the bomb.

A new sand filter is fitted to a Ju 87 B-2. The motor could be protected only insufficiently against the all-penetrating dust.

Several Ju 87 R's of StG 1 bore the emblem of the German Afrika-Korps.

Dive-bomber attacks on supply ships before the besieged fortress of Tobruk. The steamships at the top and the lower right have already been sunk.

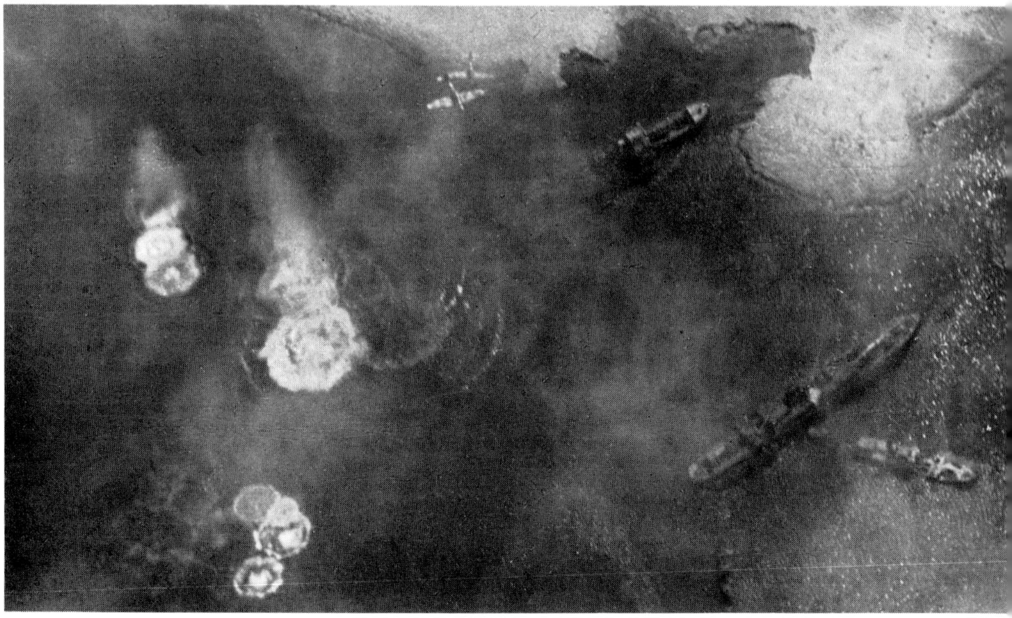

The I./StG 3 in chain formation. Even in its fast form, the Ju 87 was tail-heavy. Varying camouflage and positions of the fuselage band can be seen.

Here the group marking "S" and unit letter "L" are newly painted and can be seen clearly.

An almost new Ju 87 D-1 in tropical paint. This series had two Jericho sirens as standard equipment. The long-range tanks were used only for delivery flights.

The cabin glass of the "Dora" looked much more stylish than that of the previous model. The speed-controlled sights for the rear MG 81Z gun are still lacking; under the plexiglas cover behind the B position is the Peil G IV navigational instrument.

Instrument panel of the Ju 87 D:

1. Airscrew adjustment
2. Accelerator
3. Robot camera release
4. Weapons loading switch
5. Shot counter box
6. Instrument lighting
7. Clock
8. Battery charge indicator
9. Altimeter
10. Navigation controls
11. Contact altimeter
12. Magnetic compass
13. Instrument light regulator
14. Fuel tank switch
15. Net quick-release
16. Starter
17. Fuel gauge
18. Oil pressure gauge
19. Steering stick
20. Shutter control for bottom window
21. On-off switch for noisemaker (Jericho siren).

MG 81 Z gun in a Ju 87 D-1. The cables are the gun's lashings.

With a 700-kilogram bomb load, the commander of the III./ZG 26 takes off on a mission against the fortress of Tobruk.

A Ju 87 D-1 of StG 3 in North Africa. The unit had meanwhile introduced the S7+identification. As was customary with dive bombers, the old unit identification was retained under the wings.

A Bf 110 D-3 of the 8./ZG 26 in sand-yellow paint, escorting a cruiser of the Montecuccoli class. The MG 81 Z as defensive armament was unusual for this type of plane.

The Bf 110 E-1 planes of the III./ZG 26 were loaded with two 250-kg bombs under the fuselage and two 50-kg bombs under each wing for attacks on Tobruk. Most of the destroyers in North Africa were painted in 74/75/02 gray shades.

In a Bf 110 C-6, the MK 101 was tested in the semirigid L 101/1 mount.

In a Bf 110 E of the 8./ZG 26, this weapon was used against ships and tanks.

Servicing the FF machine gun mount of a Bf 110 D of the 9./ZG 26. The black double chevron on the nose was the traditional symbol of the destroyer.

A Bf 110 F-1 in the new desert camouflage: olive-green flecks on an ochre-brown background. The dust protector pipes on the guns can be seen.

On the Me 210, factory number 063, this new tandem bomb mounting was tested; it was then used on the planes of the III./ZG 1 in Italy in 1943.

In 1943 the 10./ZG 26 received several Ju 88 C-6 planes for escort work and submarine fighting.

While the chasers were already flying the Bf 109 F, the pursuit-bomber units of the III./JG 27 were still using the Bf 109 E-4/B because of its cannon armament. The planes bore eye-catching markings, so as not to be shot down by their own anti-aircraft guns or chasers during low-level flights: yellow motor cowlings, white fuselage bands and rudders, and white tops and bottoms of their control surfaces and wing tips.

At the end of 1942, Hs 129 B-1 and B-2 fighter planes arrived in North Africa for use by the 4. and 8./Sch.G 2. The planes were painted in 79 sand tan with green flecks and light blue identifying letters.

The plane in the lower picture is flown by a group captain, who has a sheet-metal pennant on the antenna staff. The plane also has a white chevron before the identifying letter.

A factory-new Fw 109 F-2, ready to be ferried to Italy.

The common identifying marks of the F-1 to F-3 were the external sand filters.

Unusual camouflage of an Fw 190 A-3 of the III./SKG 10: diagonal stripes in sand tan 79 and olive green 80. San Pietro, Sicily, 1943.

An Fw 190 pursuit bomber of SG 4 in Italy, 1944, the pursuit-bomber version of the A-7 with an MG 131 over the motor.

The G-3 could be recognized by the removal of the MG 131 and the disguised shot holes.

The 79/80 camouflage colors were also sprayed over the crosses on the control surfaces and wings, and the white identifying band was likewise half covered.

The Fw 190 G-3 series could be recognized by the Fw bomb racks under the wings. SG 4, Italy, 1944.

The SC 250 bomb with nose ring was used to attack landing craft.

An Fw 190 F-8 captured by American troops. This series no longer had sand filters. The strengthened rear armor required the arched cabin glass.

The whole plane was certainly originally painted with the light green meander pattern; after the motor was changed, its cowling was not painted to match.

Perfect camouflage for low-level action on bright nights, on a Ju 87 D-7 of NSGr 7 in Italy: light gray meander patterns on a dark gray background.

The two-seat Fw 190 A-8/U 1 planes of SG 151 were sometimes also used for night fighting missions. It was the second man's job to watch for enemy night fighters.

Above: Bf 110 G-2 and G-4 planes of the II./ZG 1 as heavy pursuit bombers, in Italy, 1943.

Center: A Bf 110 G-4 of the II./ZG 1 in southern Italy. It was planned to use the destroyers as pursuit bombers in the event of an Allied landing.

Right: After Italy surrendered, several Reggiane Re 2001's were to be rebuilt as pursuit bombers, but they never turned up in the troops' records.

The Bottomless Barrel: Army Support on the Eastern Front, 1941-1945

On June 22 Germany attacked the Soviet Union along a 1600 kilometer front. The initial successes could not hide the fact that the close-combat forces, and the Luftwaffe in general, were simply not capable of surviving a war of attrition. In Air Fleet 5, 42 Ju 87 B or R planes of the IV./LG 1 supported the attack on Murmansk. All other close-combat planes were with Air Fleet 2 to support the Army Group Center: two groups from StG 2 with 83 Ju 87's in Richthofen's Eighth Flying Corps, under whose command there were also the Do 17's of KG 2, the II./LG 2 with four units, and ZG 26 with two. The Second Flying Corps of Loerzer included StG 77 with 122 planes and SKG 210 (the former EGr 210), which consisted since April of two Bf 110 groups and one with Bf 109 E planes.

As in the blitz campaigns of 1939-40, the dive bombers and fighters again played a major role in the victories of the summer of 1941. The losses were relatively small, since the crews were well-trained and confident of their planes' performance. Old veterans went into air battles against Russian fighters without hesitation in their Hs 123 or Ju 87 planes. Only the 4th to 6th units of LG 2, equipped with Bf 109 E-7's, suffered heavy losses. On account of repeated motor and landing gear damage, there were seldom more than three planes per unit ready for action, whereas the tenth unit, equipped with Hs 123's, had at least nine planes ready.

Of the countless missions flown by the dive bombers, only those of StG 2 against the Baltic Sea Fleet at Kronstadt, which put many of them out of commission, can be noted here. The sea battle over Kirkenes, in which the 12./LG 1 shot down five "Swordfish" torpedo bombers from the aircraft carrier "Glorious", is not well known.

The thoroughly poor planning on the one hand, which included a decrease in aircraft production in the summer of 1941, and the high operational losses on the other, led in the late autumn of 1941 to a rapid decrease in combat readiness: in November of 1941 the Luftwaffe did not get any of its 230 Ju 87's into the air on the eastern front. When the Russian counter-offensive began in December, the Luftwaffe was exhausted. To avoid a catastrophe, anything that could carry bombs was thrown into the battle: Bf 109 F's of the chaser groups, Fi 156, Hs 126 and the few Fw 189 planes of the short-range reconnaissance units.

The situation was exacerbated by the fact that several Ju 87 units had been transferred back to Germany to be reequipped with the new Ju 87 D-1 planes. The powerplant performance of the Jumo 211 had been increased to 1420 HP in the "Dora", the body and cabin had been improved aerodynamically, the defensive power was increased considerably by the use of the MG 81 Z gun. This new type could carry bombs as heavy as the SD 1800. Even the SKG 210 had been withdrawn for reequipping with the Me 210 at Lechfeld, and was renamed ZG 1. And only ruins of ZG 26 remained; as a unit, it ceased to exist.

In any case, the front could be brought to a standstill. Reequipping with the Ju 87 D-1 could be speeded up, and the new ZG 1 and 2 could be set up in Germany as pursuit-bomber groups with Bf 110 F-4 and G-2 planes (since the Me 210 proved to be a total failure). The 1942 summer offensive had the goal of reaching the Volga and the Caucasus. In the process, the army was supported by StG 1, 2, 77, Sch.G 1, ZG 1 and ZG 2 as close-combat groups, but the chasers also had to serve as pursuit bombers here and there. The StG units had meanwhile received some of the D-2 planes, which had couplings for pulling DFS 230 freight gliders. The dive bombers were supposed to take their ground personnel along in gliders in fast transfers. In May of 1942 the D-3 series also reached the troops, with their motors, radiators and cabins protected by extra armor.

At year's end the fighting concentrated around Stalingrad, whose factories, actual fortresses of concrete, could greatly withstand the dive-bomber attacks. Despite the hardest fighting, they could not make it possible for the army to take the city. And as the winter began, the strength of the flying groups was exhausted, as it had been a year before. The Russian counter-offensive found no more air-bound enemies that could stop it at the right time. Since the entire front was weakening, the Luftwaffe set up harassment units after the Russian model, at first called auxiliary close-combat groups; thirteen groups in all of Air Fleets 1, 4 and 6 were equipped with the oldest planes: He 46, Ar 66, Go 145, Fw 58, which had been equipped with makeshift bomb racks and dropping mechanisms for light splinter bombs. The flying personnel were scrounged up from schools, air service units, ferrying groups and courier units. The main criterion was that the pilot had a blind-flying license. The auxiliary might-fighter groups too, as well as the destroyer groups of the battle squadrons that were equipped with the Ju 88 C-6, were thrown into the ground-war action.

As 1942 gave way to 1943, Sch.G 1 had its Bf 109's replaced by Fw 190's, and in fact the U 3 fighter version, which was renamed retroactively in April of 1943 to F-1 through F-3, depending on the model, but until April of 1943 there were still Bf 109 E-7's in use with Sch.G 1. The fourth and eighth groups of Battle Squadrons 1 and 2 were given the Hs 129 B-1; such Hs 123's as were still usable were overhauled and sent back to the eastern front. The last Bf 110's disappeared from Russia in July of 1943 with the transfer of ZG 1 to Italy.

In February of 1943 that veteran among fighter pilots, Lieutenant Colonel Weiss, was ordered to set up a test unit for tank fighting. Tested and compared were the following planes: Ju 87 D-1 with a BK 3.7 under each wing, Hs 129 with MK 103, BK 3.7, BK 5 and 7.5, as well as a Ju 88 with BK 7.5. Only the Hs 123 could go into production immediately, although its MK 103 could only destroy a tank if its shells hit at a favorable angle. The Ju 88 P with the absolutely deadly BK 7.5 proved to be much too ponderous. Besides, the muzzle gas pressure was so strong that the bow of the plane was pushed in and the propeller blades bent. The best compromise solution was thought to be the Ju 87 with BK 3.7. 199 planes of this type, designated G-1, were contracted for. Even so, the Ju 88 was to be experimented with further, for the formation of a tank-attack squadron, with one group each of Ju 88 P, Ku 87 G and Hs 129, was planned for the end of 1943. When the Wehrmacht began its last great offensive in the summer of 1943, operation "Citadel", supported by the massed deployment of the Ju 87, there were only five tank-fighting units equipped with Hs 129's: the 4. and 8./Sch.G 1 and Sch.G 2 and the PzJ.St/JG 51. When during this battle the Red Army made an armored advance into the unsecured flank of the Second SS Tank Army, the Hs 129's of the two battle squadrons were able to wipe out a Soviet tank brigade. An old legend must be done away with here once and for all: that of the unreliability of the Hs 129. Though it may be true of the B-1 version in Africa, in Russia the readiness of these planes amounted to 60% and more of the first-line strength.

In the autumn of 1943 the close-combat groups were fully reorganized. Formerly, the dive bombers were subordinate to the Inspector of Combat Planes, the fighters to the "General of the Pursuit Planes", and there was also a commander of the tank chasers. In order to make an end of all this confusion, in September of 1943 the position of "General of the Fighter Planes" was set up, and all StG and Sch.G units were made subordinate to it. On October 18, all of these units were renamed "SG", with the exception at first of the I./StG 2 and II./StG 77.

These units were supposed to be uninvolved in reequipping from the Ju 87 to the Fw 190. The Hs 129 units were combined into the IV.(Pz)/SG 9 (the other groups were to be set up later with Ju 87 and Ju 88 planes, which never happened). On the same date the harassing units became night-fighter units without any of their equipment changing at first.

Only at the end of 1943 did the production of Fw fighters get into full swing. Until March of 1944 it was the F-3, which then was superseded by the F-8. Still the needs of the troops could not be met, so that all of the groups also had fighters of the Fw 190 A-5 to A-8 series, which had been modified to serve as pursuit bombers. On the other hand, the pursuit bombers with increased range, the G series, never saw service on the eastern front. The Ju 87 D was used only by the I./SG 1, III./SG 2 and III./SG 77, then as the Ju 87 G tank chaser by the tenth units of SG 1, 2, 3 and 77. The D-model belonged to the D-5 series, which differed from its predecessors chiefly in having MG 151 wing guns. The older D-1 and D-3 planes were rebuilt into D-7 or D-8 night fighters, recognizable by their voluminous exhaust-flame dampers.

The night-fighting units in particular were expanded further. The NSGr 8 (with Ju 87's) was in Finland in 1944, the NSGr 10 (formed of personnel from Airborne Squadron 1) in the Southeast, while Latvian and Estonian volunteers were included in NSGr 11 and 12, which used, among other planes, the original He 50 dive bomber and the Fokker CV.

Although the aircraft used by the German combat aviators improved steadily, their numbers and their degree of combat-readiness increased, the other side became even stronger. The close-combat fliers suffered most from erroneous planning: instead of crippling the Russian tank factories with long-range bombers, the individual tanks had to be shot down on the front, with high personal and material losses. Outstanding individual achievements could prevent the collapse as little as the introduction of new weapons, such as the Panzerschreck and Panzerblitz antitank rockets. Although the FW 190 planes equipped with them had to fly slowly, until they could practically feel the tanks, and so were exposed to effective anti-aircraft fire, remarkable successes could be scored. By the beginning of 1945, every fighter squadron had a Panzerblitz unit.

Shortly before the war ended, several examples of the Si 204 E light night fighter plane turned up at the front. It had been developed from the courier plane, had two fixed MG 151 guns plus one MG 131 in a rotating turret as defensive weapons, and could carry 500-kilogram bombs. The IV.NJG 2 was renamed NSGr 30 in February of 1945, when it was in the process of being reequipped with the Si 204. But it still flew most of its night missions with Ju 88 G-1 and G-6 planes. The night pursuit pilots of NJG 5 were also used for night fighting, except for the aces.

It is noteworthy that the Gauleiter of East Prussia intended to set up a Volkssturm unit at the end of 1944, which would be thrown into the fight with any available holders of a pilot's license flying the most unsuitable small sport planes, such as the Bü 131 and Klemm L 20.

By war's end, all the tank-chaser units and almost all the fighter and night-fighter groups on the eastern front were brought together, and met defeat there.

In the summer of 1941 the dive bombers fought as they had that spring, opening the way for the army—in formation dive attack or diagonal flight against individual targets.

A Ju 87 B-2 of the 1./StG 2 is refueled. The planes of this unit had yellow-orange motor cowlings during part of 1941. The Jericho sirens came into general use only during and after the Balkan campaign.

Right page:
Upper left: To increase the firepower in operations against ground targets, the TO of KG 51 had five MG 17 guns installed in the bow of this Ju 88 A-5.

Right: The two MG 17 guns installed over the motor of this Hs 123 could only be used against troops.

Below: Ju 87 B-2 planes in low-level flight over a tank servicing facility.

The powerplant of the Ju 87 B-2 was started by a flywheel starter that a crewman had to turn with a crank.

An unusual combination of bombs: under the right wing are two SC 50, under the fuselage and left wing one SD 250 each.

Lieutenant General Wolfram, Baron von Richthofen, commanding general of the Eighth Flying Corps.

First Lieutenant Druschel led the fourth unit in the summer of 1941; the photo shows him as commander of the II./Sch.G.1 in 1942.

With his Bf 109 F, Sergeant Pichler of the 7./JG 77 also sank two ships.

The calm mood of this picture is deceiving—in 1941 the Hs 123 flew more missions per plane than any other model of airplane.

The motor cowlings, painted yellow during the Balkan campaign, were green on top again in 1941.

In 1941 too, most squadrons were using several Bf 109 E-4 and E-7 planes as pursuit bombers, as they were superior to the F series thanks to the guns in their wings. This is the plane of the II./JG 54's group adjutant, Lieutenant Steindl, near Leningrad in the autumn of 1942.

The Bf 110 E of ZG 1 were used in Russia in 1941 with much success as heavy pursuit bombers.

A Bf 109 E-7/B of the II.(S)/LG 2. This type had armor plates on the cabin sides and a front window of armor glass.

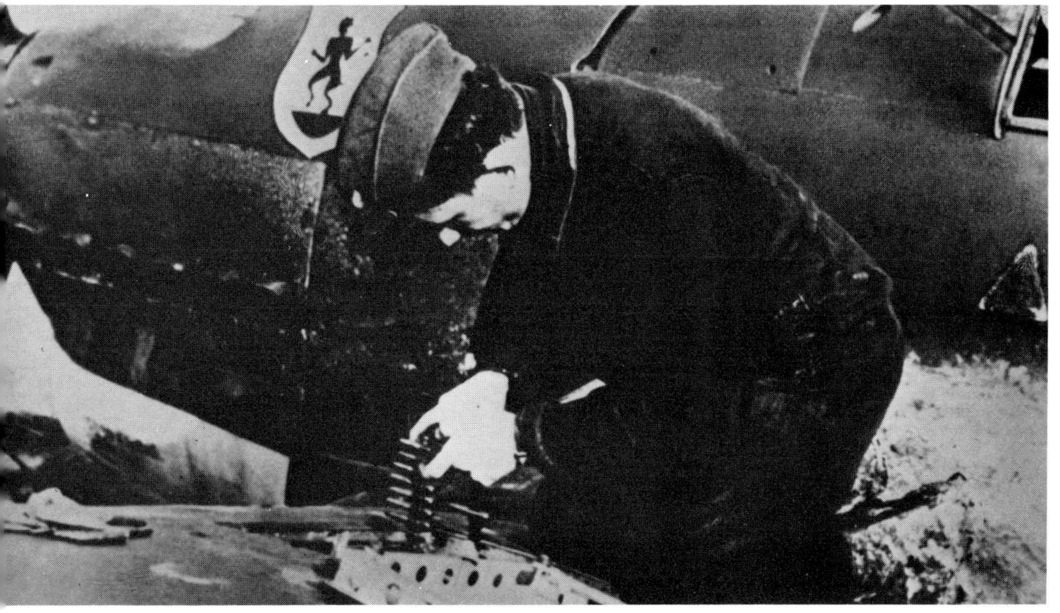

After six months on the eastern front, nothing remains of the once well-kept exteriors of such planes as this Ju 87 B of the 9./StG 2.

Ordnance service men of StG 2 await the return of the planes.

Even an ancient Bf 109 E-1 flew with the II./LG 2, loaded here with four 50-kilogram bombs.

Left: Hs 123 in winter paint, which could be washed off. The effects of thirty-below-zero temperatures on the crews of the open planes can scarcely be described.—Right: First Lieutenant Georg Dörffel, Captain of the 5.(S)/LG 2, stands before his Bf 109 E-7 "White U". His face shows the effects of the hard fighting during the summer of 1941—Dörffel was just 27 years old!

A Bf 109 E-7 of the II.(S)/LG 2 in the spring of 1941.

During the first winter warfare in Russia, the Luftwaffe used any plane that could carry bombs, even Fi 156 and Hs 126.

Two Fi 156 C's on an armed reconnaissance flight ahead of a German armored advance, December 1941.

In 1941 a test unit in the East was to be equipped with the BV 141, which like the Fw 189 could carry four bombs.

Overhauled and newly painted, the Hs 123's of Sch.G. 1 are ready for the summer offensive on the southern front.

This Hs 123 still has an annular sight in front of the front window.

In the spring of 1942 the Ju 87 D-1 reached the troops.

The new oil cooler with the lever-activated vents that were closed during a dive.

The underside of the fuselage and wings, with bomb carriers and swivels at right and a water cooler to the left.

Details of the engine cowling. Before the supercharger intake of the flap that was closed for diving. The manufacturer's trade mark is on the exhaust stubs.

Position C of the Ju 87:

The defensive weapon of the Ju 87 B: MG 15 machine gun, firing speed 1020 shots per minute, in an unarmored lens mount.

The MG 81 Z of the Ju 87 D in a rolling mount, with an armored apron behind it, had a firing speed of 3200 shots per minute.

Almost new Ju 87 D-1 planes of the III./StG 1. One can see the changed mounting of the bomb swivel. The rear wheel cover of the machine below is obviously only primed.

The ZG 1, newly formed at the beginning of 1942, used Bf 110 F or E planes, plus Bf 109 E-7's in its third group. The S9 numbering of the SKG 210 was retained.

A Ju 87 D-1 of the commander of the I./StG 2, Captain Bruno Dilley, numbered T6+CB. A special feature is the commander's sight before the group marking.

A brand new, still "anonymous" Ju 87 D-2 with a tow hook behind the tail wheel. I./StG 2, summer of 1942.

An emergency takeoff of the 3./StG 1 from a dusty field on the Russian steppes.

Left page: A Ju 87 D-1 of the 7./StG 1, summer of 1942.

110 The Ju 87's of the StG 77 staff flight could be recognized by the white diagonal stripes on their rudders.

Men of a Luftwaffe construction company pose with a Ju 87 D-3 of the II./StG 2 that had to land with its oil tank empty.

Captain Janke, Captain of the 5./StG 2, returns from his 200th combat mission. The additional armor of the Ju 87 D-3 is clearly seen.

An Fw 189 wants to land on an auxiliary airfield. A sight cloth is spread out, and a Cossack horseman takes a flare to show the pilot the wind direction.

The "Storks" used to pick up crash-landed crews also bore assault symbols and the fighter-plane triangle. In the foreground is the wreck of an Hs 129.

A Ju 87 of the III./StG 1 in action against a single target, with three 250-kilogram bombs; the outer ones have so-called Dinort staffs, tubes to protect the detonators.

The same plane armed to attack area targets: 50-kilogram bombs under the wings, drop containers for light splinter bombs under the fuselage. The group emblems are under the wings.

The WB 81 weapon holder with three twinned MG 81 guns on the ETC of a Ju 87 D-3.

Combat briefing before the attack on the Kertsch peninsula, May 1942. From right to left: First Lieutenants Druschel and Frank, both of Sch.G 1, and General von Richthofen's adjutant.

On October 30, 1942 Major Dr. Kupfer, II./StG 2, received the congratulations of his group after his 500th combat mission.

Splendid "echelon right" formations, above with the II./StG 2, below the II./StG 77. The T6+HM in the upper picture is a Ju 87 D-3.

 A formation of Ju 87 D-1 and D-2 planes make a turn to the left together.

A "Dora" is escorted by a Bf 109 F-4 of the I./JG 51.

Dive bombers are loaded with SC 50 and SC 250 explosive bombs as well as AB 250-2 drop containers. All the bombs have Jericho pipes to increase the psychological effect.

Training near the front with the replenishment echelon of Sch.G 1 at Novocherkassk in 1942. The Hs 123's bear the prewar regimental paint.

A Bf 190 E of SG 2 lands. On this plane the triangle is forward of the cross emblem.

Georg Dörffel, 5./Sch.G 1, is congratulated again.

Welcome for Dörffel (right) and Dörnbrack (left) after their 600th combat mission on August 16, 1942. I.d.M. of the commander, Captain Druschel.

Josef Menapace, adjutant of the I./Sch.G 1, preferred the indestructible Hs 123 to the Bf 109 E. In August of 1942 Menapace had 650 combat missions behind him.

Compare the well-kept training plane of the Erg./Sch.G 1 with the battered old crock of Menapace! Since the auxiliary tank could not be dropped, it was never used at the front.

Dörffel takes off. The rudder is turned in to equalize the torque of the airscrew.

Druschel's Bf 109 E-7 loaded with four bundles of 10-kilogram bombs.

Exhaust has blackened the lower half of the II./StG 77 group emblem.

Richthofen on the reviewing stand.

General von Richthofen with fighter pilot Captain Baumbach.

In combat with the Eighth Flying Corps before Sevastopol, 1942.

Flight communications officers (Flivos) lead an attack of StG 77 on a tank fortress.

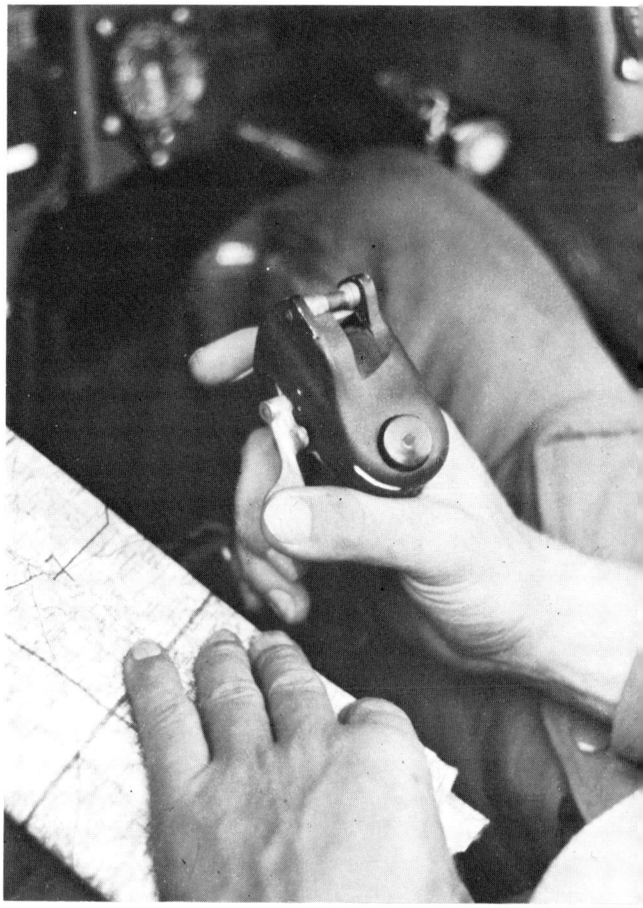

At Tarnewitz rear-view periscopes are tested on an Hs 129 B-1, possibly in connection with a gun firing to the rear.

The steering handle of the Hs 129. The pilot's thumb is on the weapon-release lever. On the handle is the bomb-release button.

Four MG 17 guns as armament set R3 under the fuselage of an Hs 129 B-1.

Hs 129 B-1 with MK 101 under its fuselage and SC 50 bombs under the wings.

"Ready to take off!" with an Hs 129 B. The rear-view mirror and 10-, 20-and 30-degree diving-angle lines on the side window are easy to see.

Hs 129 B-1 of the I./Sch.G 1, with SC 10 bundles under the wings.

What remained of ZG 1, equipped with Bf 110 G-2's, flew pursuit-bomber missions during the fighting around Stalingrad.

Left page: Since the Red Army used even the most unfavorable weather for their counteroffensives, the Ju 87's had to fly night missions even in the winter of 1942-43.

Examples of winter camouflage paint on the Ju 87 D in the winter of 1943. The plane below still has cover plates on the wings. To avoid icing, they were removed just before takeoff.

A dive-bomber attack on a concentration of Russian T-34 tanks and vehicles in a Russian village. The wheel and tread tracks are easy to see.

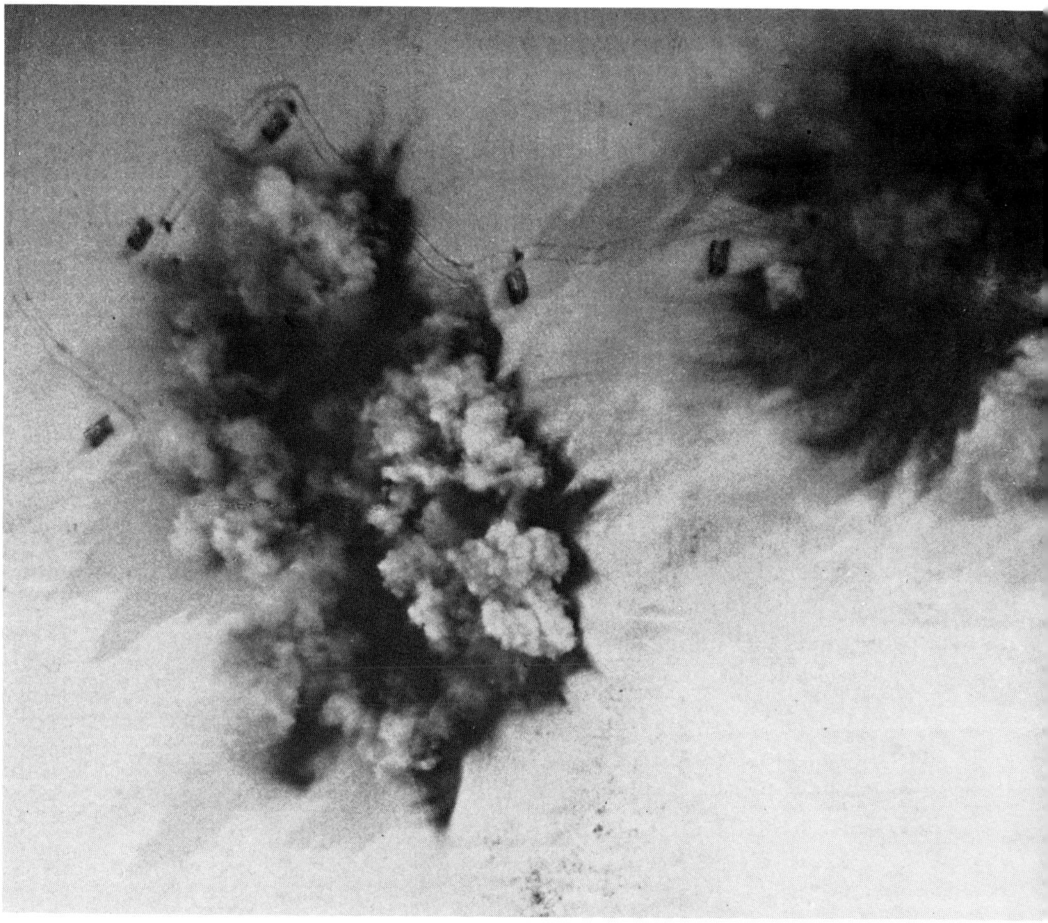

He 177 A-1 with bow-mounted MK 101. Some planes of Long-range Battle Group 2, which were sent to Stalingrad in January of 1943, were fitted with these guns to fire on Russian anti-aircraft positions.

The harassing echelon of Air Fleet 6 was equipped with several Fw 58 “leucoplast bombers”.

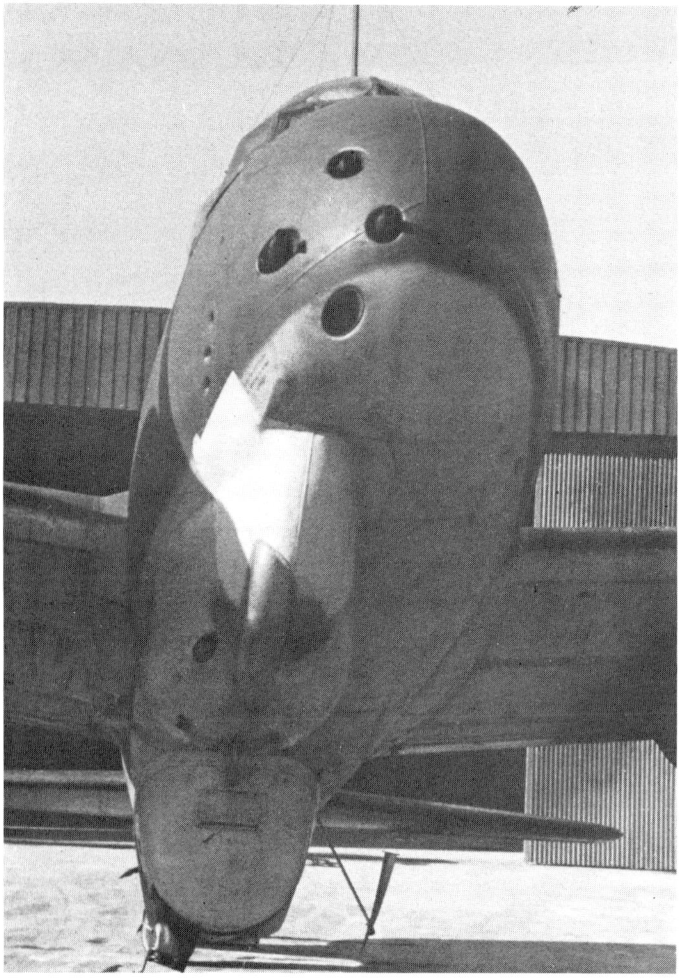

In the winter of 1943 the KG 53 was given a railroad-attacking unit equipped with Ju 88 C-6 planes.

The wing tanks of a Ju 87 D-2 are filled. This type can be recognized by the tow hook behind the tail wheel.

Several He 111 H-11 planes were turned into auxiliary night fighters by the addition of four MG 151 guns, but they were usually used against railroads.

Above: A black-painted Fw 58 C with bow armament, of the harassing echelon of Air Fleet 6.

Center: An Fw 189 guiding a Ju 87 D of StG 2.

To defend against Russian breakthroughs in the spring of 1943, any plane that could carry bombs was used.

Left: SC 50 bombs are hung on the carriers of an Fw A-2.

Deployed in columns, a Ju 87 group flies back to the landing field.

A Bf 109 F-4/R 1 of the II./JG 54 has had a saddle carrier for four 50-kilogram bombs built on and the MG 151 guns removed from the gondolas under the wings.

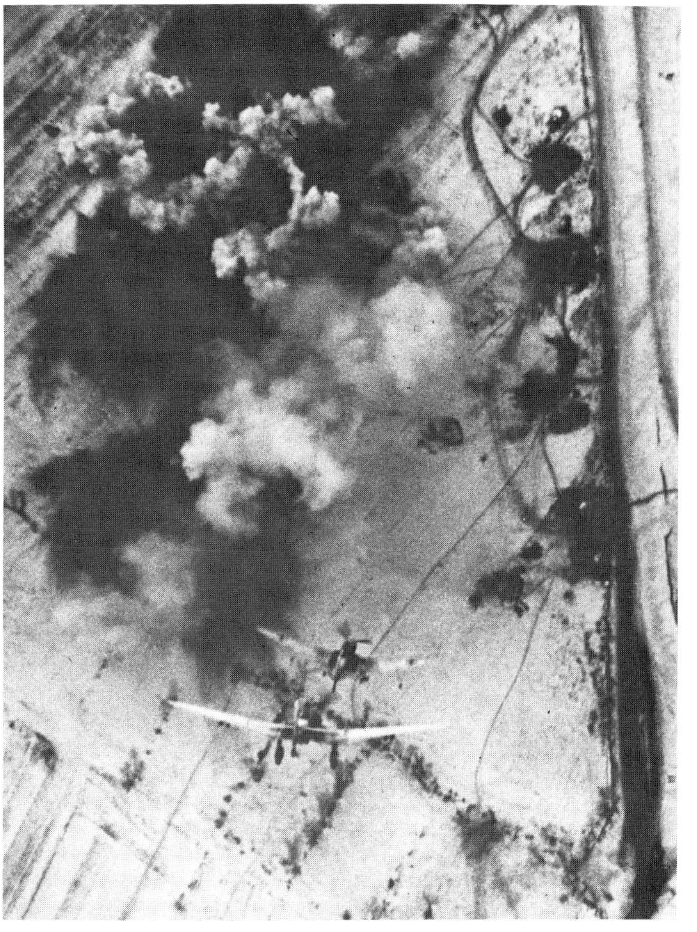

Left: A direct hit on a train. Right: an almost vertical dive on a Soviet artillery emplacement.

Weapon pits at an intersection are under fire.

On October 30, 1942 the commander of the II./StG 2, Major Dr. Kupfer, returned from his 500th combat mission in the Stalingrad area.

On February 10, 1943 First Lieutenant Rudel, with 1000 missions, leads all dive-bomber and fighter pilots. At right is his radioman, Master Sergeant Hentschel.

The Ju 88 A-13, an additionally armored fighter-plane version, whose WB 81 weapons holders fired a hail of 130 rounds per second.

In the spring of 1943 the retraining of Bf 109 crews for the Fw 190 began in ErgGr/Sch.G 1. There was still no replacement for the Hs 123.

Fighter Squadron 1 was reequipped with a colorful mixture of Fw 190 A-3, A-5 and F-2 planes.

The 14./JG 5 flew pursuit-bomber missions on the Finnish front with Fw 190 A-5/U 1 planes.

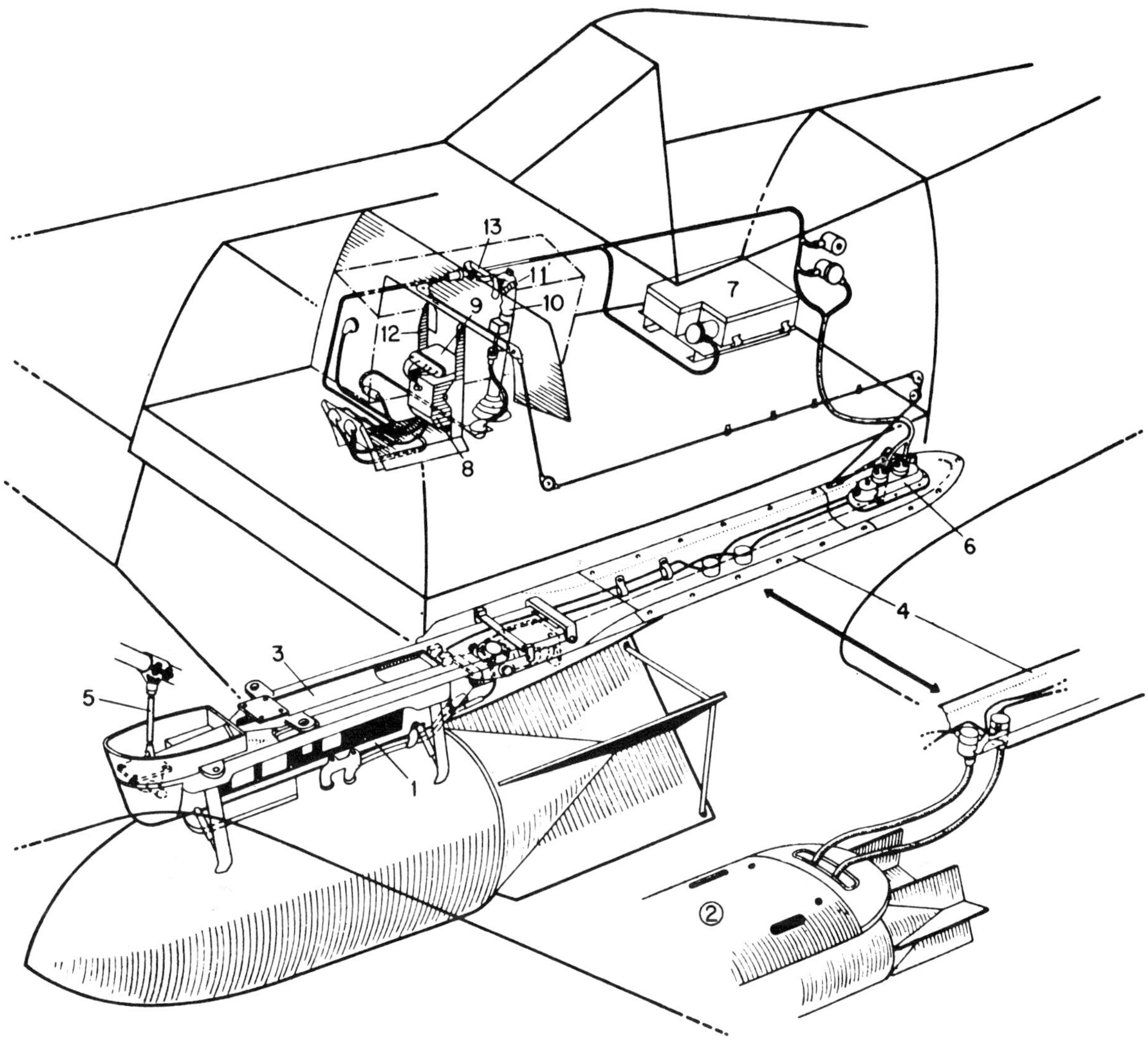

Bomb carrying and releasing mechanism of the Fw 190

1. ETC 501
2. Adapter for ER-4 hanging rack
3. ETC 501 carrier
4. Cowling
5. Support
6. Cable tube
7. ZBK (detonator battery case)
8. ZSK (detonator switch box)
9. Bomb-release indicator
10. KG 38 steering handle
11. Bomb indicator table
12. Bomb jettisoning mechanism

Since there were not enough F-series fighter planes with wing ETC units available at the beginning of 1943, A-series fighters with reduced wing armament were used, carrying the ER bomb rack with four 50-kilogram bombs or drop containers for splinter bombs under their fuselage.

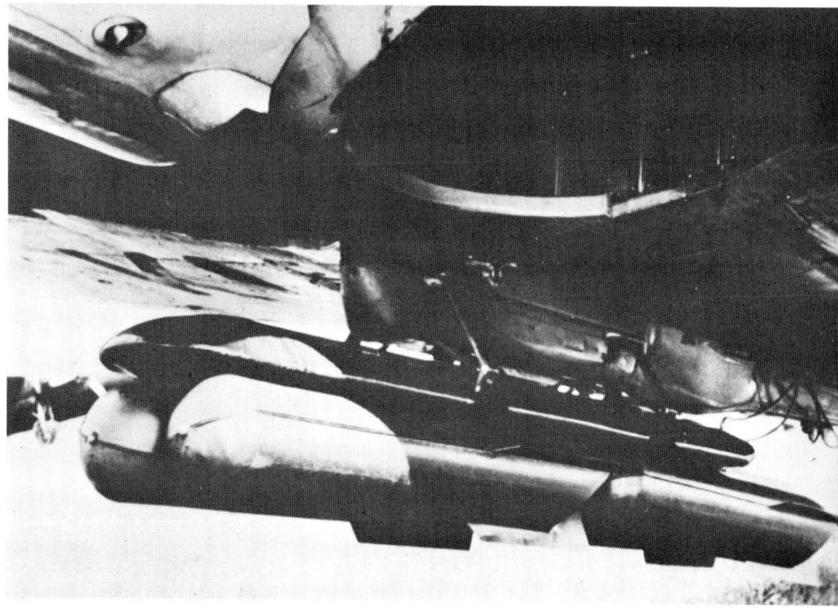

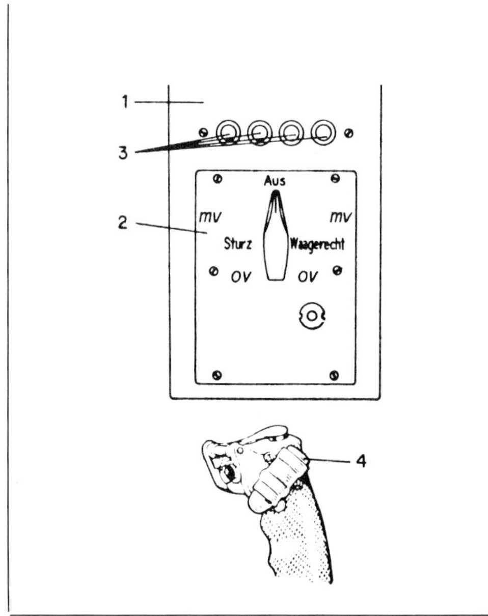

1. Bomb-dropping instrument board; 2. Detonator switch, mv: with delay, ov: without delay; 3. Indicator light for bomb dropping; 4. Bomb release button on the steering handle.

At the beginning of 1943, production of the Fw 190 A-5/U 3 was increased, and was retroactively named F-2 in April. All fighter-plane models, F-1 through F-3, had external air intakes with tropical filters. The plane in the bottom picture has an Fw carrier under its fuselage, which the G-types usually had under their wings.

Major Alfred Druschel—at age 26 sword wearer and Commodore of Sch.G 1.

In the spring of 1943 Druschel was still flying a Bf 109 E-7, which had meanwhile been painted with the commodore's chevron.

Right page: The finish of the Fw 190 A-5/U 3 or F-2 fighters was even polished at the factory.

Upper left: In 1943 only the Fw 190's of Sch.G 2 still bore the infantry assault emblem.

Upper right: The planes of the I./Sch/G 1 retained the black triangle.

Below: Druschel in his Fw 190 F-2, in the summer of 1943.

From 1942 to 1943 the markings and identification numbers of the Hs 123 were changed.

Above: The planes of the 5./(S)LG 2, with the assault emblem, echelon symbol and fighter-plane triangle behind the cross.

Center: The emblems are gone, the triangle is painted over, a bar is painted on as the symbol of the second group; on the third plane in the picture it extends into the cross emblem. Meanwhile the "timely" armament consists of SC 50 with Dinort staffs.

The plane at right may have been flown by Captain Neubert, holder of the Knight's Cross.

The airfield of StG 77 on the south Russian steppes in the summer of 1943; high woven fences had to replace the splinter boxes.

Lieutenant Gebert of the 4./StG 2 was rammed by a Russian plane and had to crash-land with damaged landing gear.

The communications planes of the fighter units also bore the infantry assault emblem.

An Fw 189 A-1 of the I.(H)/32 takes off from Kemi Airfield in Finland for an armed reconnaissance flight. In the northern sector of the eastern front, many planes were painted in olive brown and green camouflage colors. Under the fuselage are the rarely attached long ejector tubes for shell casings.

Over the airfield at Immola, Ju 87's of the IV./LG 1 gather. In the foreground is an Fw 190 A-5 of the IV./JG 5.

In the fighting around the Kuban bridgehead, Ju 87 D's of the I./StG 2 and Hs 129 B-2/R 3's of the 8./SG 1 achieved great success against Russian landing craft.

144 **Ruffer's Hs 129 B-2/R 3 after destroying eight tanks in April of 1943. The white lines on the wings helped in adjusting the landing flaps and ailerons.**

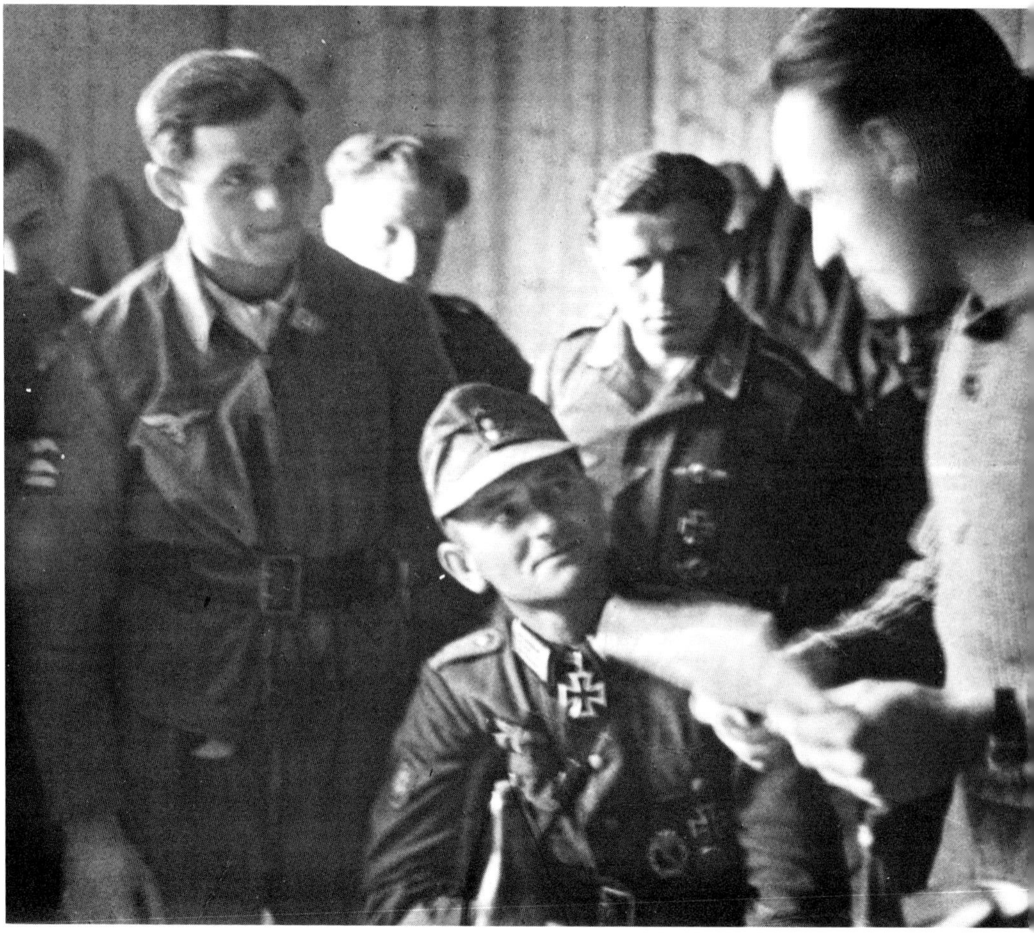

Combat briefing of the 8./Sch.G 1 with mountaineers; at left is First Lieutenant Ruffer. Kuban bridgehead, in the spring of 1943.

The twist-stabilized RZ 65 rockets for use against air and ground targets were tested thoroughly, to be sure, but never saw service with the troops.

Above: Drum firing devices under a Ju 88 A-4.

Below: Eleven single-shot devices under a Bf 110.

One group of a new tank-chaser squadron was supposed to be set up in 1943, equipped with Bf 110 G-2 day destroyers armed with the BK 3.7 gun. The empty magazine sticks out of the bottom of the cowling.

Despite balancing ballast in the rear, landings with the nose-heavy Ju 88 PV 1 were problematic.

Shooting practice with the Ju 88 PV 1. When firing in the air, the shock waves from the muzzle brake damaged the airscrews.

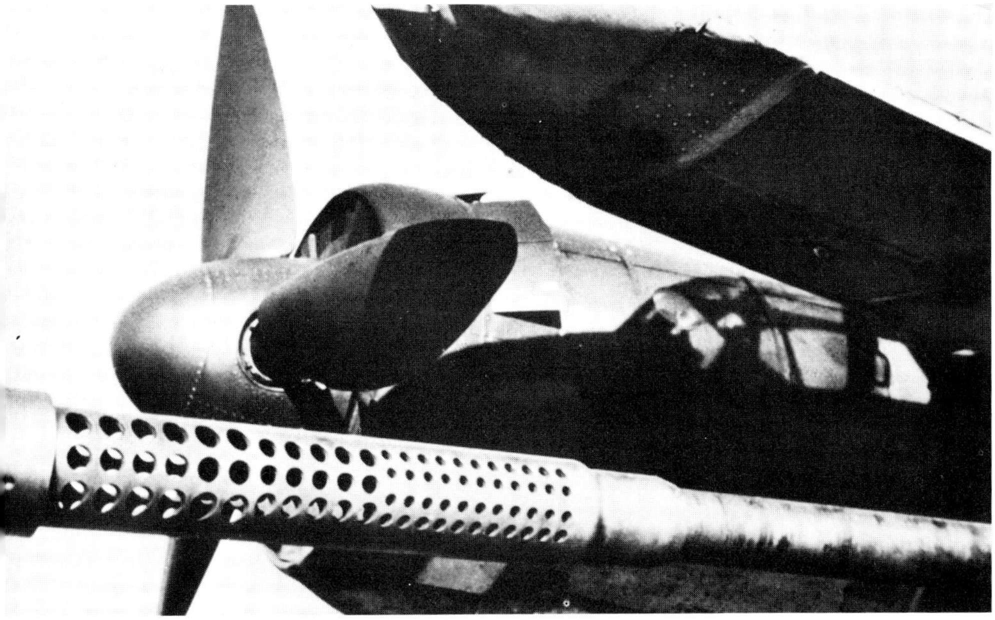

The Ju 88 P armed with the last-type BK 7.5, with its sieve-type muzzle brake. The plane retains the sheet-metal nose of the Ju 88 C.

From the Ju 87 D-3 the Ju 87 G-1 tank chaser arose, armed with two BK 3.7 guns. The opening in the cowling above the gun is an air intake for a hydraulic oil heater.

Every gun was loaded with a six-round frame, which here includes two each of incendiary-explosive, explosive and mine shells.

Details of the 7.5-cm gun of the Ju 88 P-1.

1. Barrel brace
2. Spt 12 mounting
3. Magazine
4. Spt 9 mounting
5. Compressed-air bottle
6. Compressed-air connection
7. Front mounting
8. Flap
9. Rear mounting
10. Intake box
11. Carrier
12. Loading chute
13. 7.5-cm gun attachment
14. Cradle carrier
15. Barrel cradle
16. Barrel
17. Barrel support
18. Left armor plate
19. Right armor plate
21. Muzzle brake
22. Spt 3 armor plate
23. Right armor hood
24. Armor panel
25. Left armor hood
26. Sand-protective muzzle cap

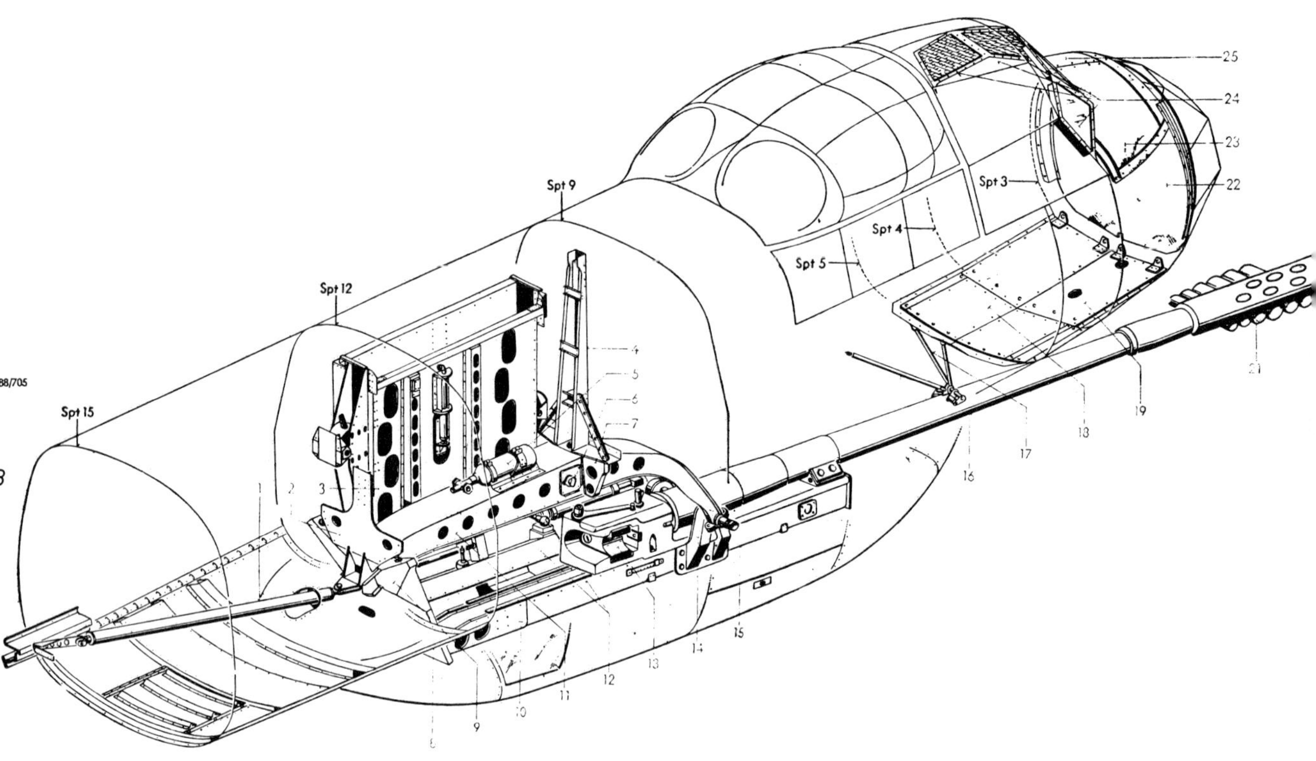

Right page: Ju 87 G-2's firing.

M531
M503
M532
M504
M508

The III./StG 2 was the first unit to receive the Ju 87 D-5 with MG 151/20 in the wings; they arrived at the end of June 1943. The belt holds alternating mine and antitank shells.

As can be seen by the varying colors of the propeller cones, Captain Rudel—in the first plane—assembled the emergency unit of the III./StG 2 out of all echelons.

The dive-bombing procedure had changed from the early days by 1943: The planes no longer turned downward nose-first, but tipped over to the left.

An air communications officer in an armored scout car observes Ju 87 D-5 planes in action.

The last large-scale operations of Ju 87 units took place in the summer of 1943, during the fighting in the central sector.

Left: An Fw 190 A-5 pursuit bomber of the I./Sch.G 1.

Center: Fw 190 F-2 planes of the II./Sch.G 1 in the Kursk offensive. The completely different identifying marks are noteworthy.

Below: From left to right: Fw 190 F-1, Fw 190 A-5/U 3 of Sch.G 1, Bf 110 G-3/R 3 of ZG 1.

Ju 87 G-2's of the tank-chaser echelon of StG 77.

In 1943 dive-bombing attacks, only bombs with detonator-protecting rods, "Dinort asparagus", were dropped. The 250-kilogram bombs had shorter rods with wider impact plates than the 50-kg. bombs.

The diving brakes of this Ju 87 D-5 have been removed.

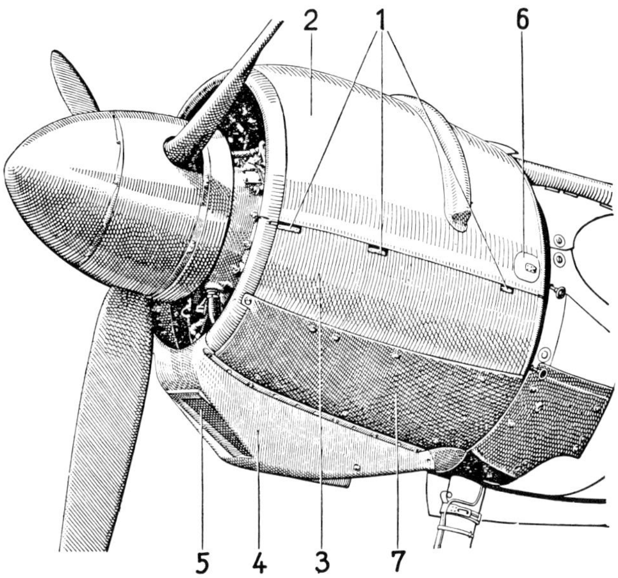

Motor cowling

1. Tension latches
2. Upper part
3. Lower part
4. Air intake shaft
5. Sand filter
6. Tension latch flap
7. Armor panel

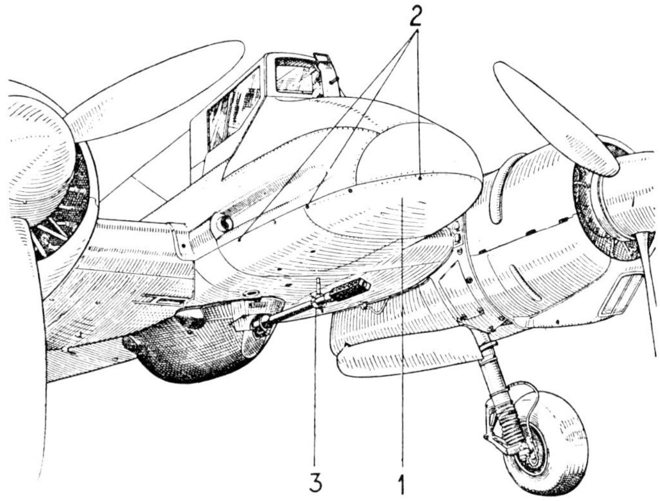

Armament set MK 103

1. Covering panel
2. Attaching screw
3. Barrel brace

Details of the Hs 129 B-2 (from the aircraft handbook)

Central fuselage section

1. Recess for MG 151
2. Flap for MG 151

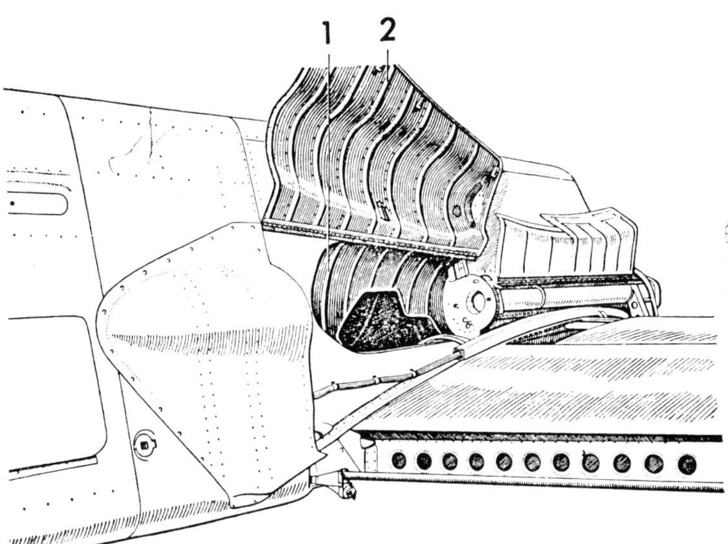

Swinging the armament set out

1. Rear lever tube

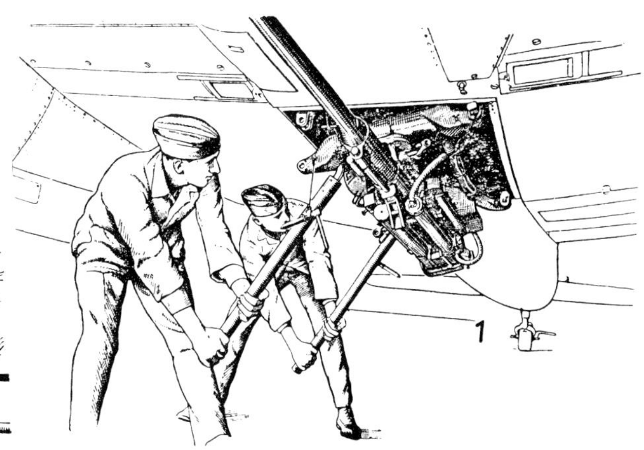

The Hs 129 B-2 was modified in 1943: short vertical exhaust pipes, rear-view mirror over the front window, and different radio antennas. But above all, most planes had the MK 101 gun replaced by the MK 103.

Upper left: Older version of the Hs 129 B-2 with the MK 101 gun. Behind the opening in the nose of the fuselage is a robot camera; the right opening is an air intake for the weapon's hydraulic heater.

Right: From factory number 300 on, the bow of the fuselage was altered.

This pilot has had his nickname painted on the nose of the fuselage.

In Luftwaffe units—here the II./Sch.G 1—the last heavy uniform vehicles were used.

Pilots of the IV./SG 9 studying the map. The Hs 129 B-2 is so weathered that the 70 and 71 green shades seem to blend into each other. The planes were equipped with the FuG 16 ZE UKW device in 1944.

In the autumn of 1943 Lieutenant Seyffardt of the 5./SG 2 returned from his 200th combat mission.

The four 50-kilogram bombs could also be dropped singly from the bomb rack.

In the autumn of 1943 Major Otto Weiss turned the command of the IV./(Pz)SG 9 over to Captain Bruno Meyer (center).

The Ju 87 D-5 with lengthened wings swinging into a diving attack. The plane in the upper picture belongs to the II./StG 1 but still bears the 6G+marking of the former III./StG 51 in 1943. A typical identifying mark of the Ju 87 was the retention of the group symbol under the wings. In addition, no bombs with Dinort rods could be carried on the fuselage bomb carriers, because of the danger of collision with the airscrew.

An Fw 190 F-2 of the II./SG 1 with red lower motor housing, but without the group bar on the fuselage. This plane's MG 17 firing openings have been covered.

Fw 190 A-5's of the SG 152 training squadron, rearmed as pursuit bombers.

An Fw 190 A-5 pursuit bomber of the I./JG 54 in the brown and olive camouflage typical of this squadron. The SC 250 bombs with heavy-caliber ring tails were used on sea targets.

Arado Ar 66 C night-fighter planes at the edge of a stubble field in Estonia in the autumn of 1943.

Servicing an Ar 66 C that has been rebuilt as a harassment plane. Note the lengthened exhaust pipe and the standard green camouflage.

First Lieutenant Specht, Echelon Captain of NSGr 3, briefs his crews. The flying personnel here consisted mainly of flight instructors.

Meanwhile the ordnance men attach AB 23 drop containers that hold 23 SD 1 splinter bombs.

A Go 145 of NSGr 3 is fueled. Sight lines have been painted on the black fuselage.

An emergency column ready for action. The rear plane carries BL C 50 flare bombs, the front one a Russian 100-kilogram bomb.

A Go 145 about to take off. These flare planes usually flew as two-seaters, and the observer was often armed with a machine pistol, with which he opened fire on ground targets as in World War I days.

The group adjutant of NSGr, First Lieutenant Doye, and his Ar 66 C, U9+EA, loaded with captured 100-kilogram bombs.

Above: Fw 190 A-5, F-2 and F-3 of SG 2 in the autumn of 1943. When the mud season began, the wheel covers were removed to avoid mud solidifying in them, jamming the wheels and causing turnovers.

Center: An Fw 190 A-5/U 1 at the fueling station of the 5./SG 2 in Crimea, in the autumn of 1943.

Right: The "moving van" of the II./SG 2, October 1943. Second from left is Fritz Seyffardt, who later won the Knight's Cross.

An Ar 66 C of a night-fighter group. The upper sides had been covered with winter camouflage paint that would wash off.

A Ju 87 D-5 of a group commander, with a green propeller cone. The Jericho sirens were no longer used on the D-5.

With the help of a portable heater unit, the powerplant of a Ju 87 D-5 is warmed up.

Above: Bf 109 G-6 planes of the II./JG 51 staff before a fighter mission.

Center: The 2./NSGr 11 was equipped with Fokker CV's captured in Denmark in 1940. The flying personnel of this group consisted of Estonian volunteers.

Right: A stack of SC 50 bombs before a Ju 87 D-5 of SG 5 in the winter of 1943-44. The exhaust has blackened the white winter camouflage on the fuselage sides. Bombs with detonator distance rods were not needed when the ground was frozen hard in winter.

These pictures show the results of a night-fighter attack on troop quarters.

Compared with the white-painted Ar 66 (at the upper left and in the middle of the picture) and the Ju 88, the dark night fighter planes look like "flies on a tablecloth".

The NSGr 11 was formed out of Reconnaissance Group 127 in October and equipped with He 50's.

An Fw 190 A-3/U 1 of JG 5 in Finland during the winter of 1943-44.

In the winter of 1943-44 the reequipping of the former dive-bomber squadrons with the Fw 190 began, though generally they were just A-5 and A-6 planes equipped with fuselage ETC's.

Above: The pursuit bombers of the 14./JG 5 bore identifying numerals like the fighters.

Center: On a very weathered Fw 190 A-5 of the II./SG 2, a glowing new white identifying letter has been painted. Crimea, end of 1943.

Right: To make cold starting easier, gasoline is mixed into the oil; it vaporizes when the motor warms up.

Congratulations for their thousandth missions: Major Henze, Commander of the I./SG 77, at Uman on February 26, 1944.

Major Friedrich Lang, III./SG 1, on March 7, 1944. At right next to Lang is his radioman Alois Berndl. Lang and Henze received the oak leaves for their achievements; Berndl received the Knight's Cross.

174 **The NSGr 1 flew these He 46 planes while with Air Fleet 1 in the northern sector. The black and green fuselages of the planes were black on the undersides of the wings as well as the fuselage. The tops of the wings show an unusual pattern, with areas of 71 green and 02 gray.**

The night fighter planes often flew their first missions even before sundown, utilizing the low-lying sun at their backs. The crews of their Ar 66 C's probably belonged to the Latvian NSGr 12.

From right to left: Lieutenant Colonel Beushausen, Commander of NSGr 3, First Lieutenant Duye and Master Sergeant Belloff, holder of the Knight's Cross; his name is on the covering of the third plane from the right.

The night fighter men used up leftovers: Above, SD 2 splinter bombs under an He 46;

Below, French 20-kilogram explosive bombs on a Go 145. After the lid was released, the 2-kilogram splinter bombs separated and slid along the shaft until they were held by its thickened end. The bombs were thus braked to their falling speed.

A night-fighter column usually included a flare plane that lit up the target with flare cascades. Here are two ejector tubes under a Go 145.

The He 46 could carry four 50-kilogram bombs, two each under the fuselage and the wing struts.

The He 46 planes of NSGr 4 bore the unit identification 1K either before or after the cross emblem.

Until the spring of 1944, the Fw 190 F-3 still had ETC units under its wings. As of January 1944 the planes were produced without external intake shafts or wing ETC's.

Above: The NSGr 7 flew Fiat CR 42's. The unit was formed in July of 1944 out of the Croatian short-range reconnaissance echelon.

Center: As in the other parts of the Luftwaffe, the flying personnel of the fighter groups got younger all the time, as can be seen clearly by their faces.

Left: The night-fighter version of the Ju 87 D-5 was the D-8, equipped with exhaust flame dampers and muzzle fire dampers on the MG 151 barrels.

A single-seat Ar 66 C of NSGr 30, painted white on its upper surfaces for safe recognition.

Thick winter clothing was urgently needed in the open cockpits of the night fighter planes.

During the snow-free months, the night fighter planes were painted completely black; even the swastika on the rudder was painted over. This is a Go 145 of NSGr 3.

In propaganda photos of 1944 one no longer sees Hs 129 B-2 planes with MK 101 guns; in reality, numerous planes were still armed with them at the end of 1944. This plane bears a very weathered winter paint job—in midsummer!

Very practical winter camouflage of Hs 129 B-2/R 3 planes of the IV./SG 9. The chalk inscriptions on the propeller blades of the plane below refer to a recently completed powerplant replacement.

182 As of October 1943, the IV./SG 9 was the only front unit using the Hs 129. The planes were usually armed with the MK 103.

Left: Major Dr. Otte, Commander of the third group. Right: Awarding the Knight's Cross to Captain Kurt Lau, I./SG 2, and Sergeant Meyering of the fourth echelon.

A parade on the occasion of the 100,000th combat mission of SG 2 "Immelmann" on April 6, 1944, at Husi airfield, Rumania.

Senior General Dessloch and the Squadron Commodore, Lieutenant Colonel Stepp, inspect the third echelon, at whose right end First Lieutenant Bauer stands.

On May 8, 1944 the SG 77 recorded its 100,000th combat mission.

The Air Fleet Chief, General Seidemann, in conversation with the Commodore, Lieutenant Colonel Bruck.

In 1944 Ju 87 D-3 and D-5 were rebuilt into D-7 and D-8 night fighters; their most noticeable identifying marks were the long exhaust flame dampers. These NSGr 5 planes in Romania have their identifying marks painted over in black, with the exception of the aircraft identification letter. The undersides of their fuselages and wings were also painted black.

The target marker of a fighter group. Under its wings this Ju 87 D-5 carries the SC 50 with Dinort rod plus an ejector tube for flares or smoke bombs. Under the fuselage is an AB 250 drop container.

Left: The vibrations of the MK 103 barrel while firing were supposed to be reduced by a restraining ring, which the ordnance man is just fastening. Right: Details of the cabin armoring of Captain Ruffer's Hs 129 B-2.

At the beginning of July 1944, Captain Ruffer, Captain of the 10.(Pz)/SG 9, had shot his seventieth tank. Captain Ruffer fell on July 16, 1944, during the Russian large-scale offensive in the central sector.

With just two 50-kilogram bombs under its wing ETC's, this Fw 190 F-3 takes off on an uneconomical long-range mission.

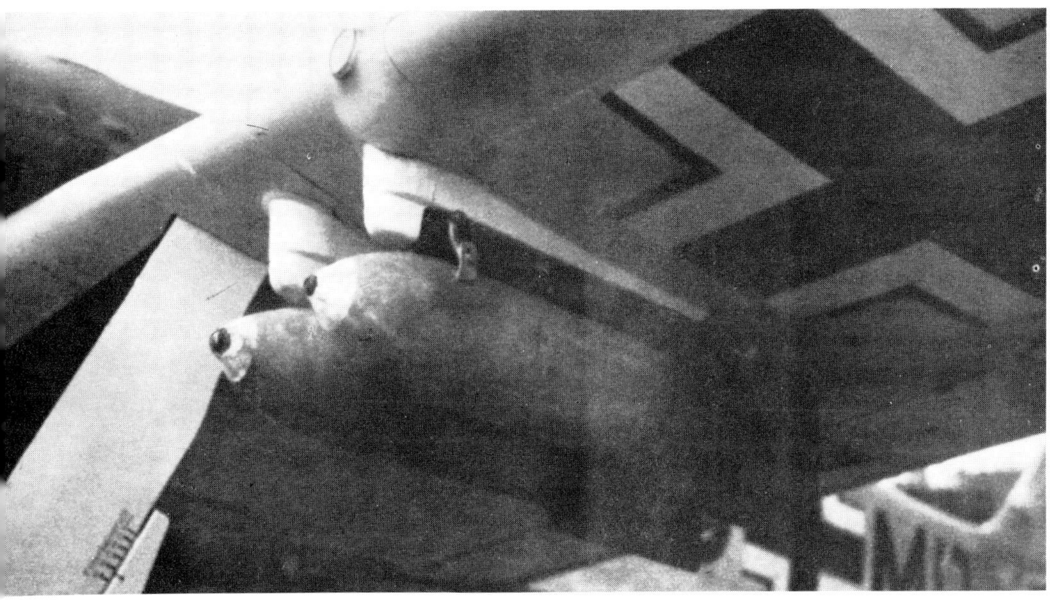

ETC 71 for 50-kilogram bombs on the model plane for the F-8 series. The robot camera, which was otherwise built into the inner wing, is mounted here at the shot aperture of the removed MG 151.

The first Fw 190 F-8's that reached SG 2 in the spring of 1944 still had external air intakes. The bombs under the wings could be dropped individually from this type.

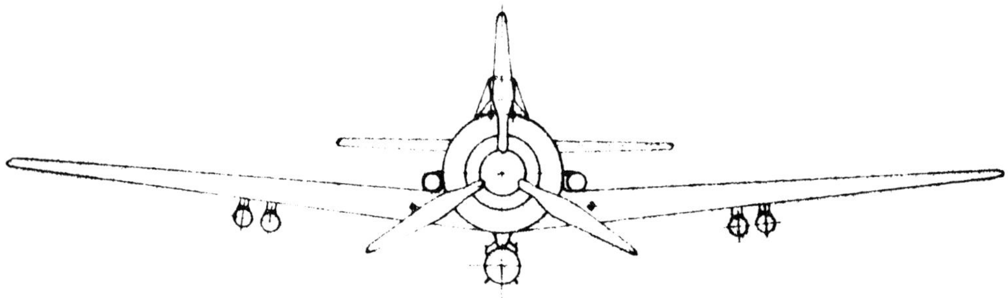

	Fuselage	Inner Wing	Outer Wing
	2 MG 17	2 MG 151	—
Armament	900	250	4 x ETC 50
Attachments	ETC 501		4 x SC 50
Bomb Load	SC 250		
Fuel Supply	410 kg		
Takeoff Weight:	4790 kg		

With this payload the Fw 190 F-3 had a calculated range of approximately 630 kilometers.

Deceptive late-summer idyll on the airfield of the 3./SG 3, probably in Courland. It is interesting that the pursuit bomber bears the unit marking of the StG 3: S7+EL.

The 250-round magazines for the MG 151/20 0f the Fw 190 F-2 were pushed into the fuselage from below; thus the fuselage ETC had to have its flap opened.

Rebuilding an Fw 190 F-2 under the most primitive conditions.

The Fw 190 F-3 was basically identical to the A-6. In order to withstand air battles with the Russian fighters without dropping its bombs prematurely, its pilots often did without bombs on the wing ETC's.

An AB 250 drop container with thirty SD 4 splinter bombs. The Fw 190 F-8 was delivered in 1944 with only fuselage ETC's; the wing ETC's were available as armament sets.

Fw 190 F-8 planes with full loads of 450 kilograms of bombs. This model had three MG 131 guns in the fuselage; the bombs under the wings could be dropped simultaneously or singly.

Every battle group had its own style of painting the identifying marks; the II./SG 4 also put the identifying letter on the motor cowling. These Fw 190 F-8's were painted splendidly: yellow on the rudder, fuselage, wing tips, armor ring and propeller cone, which had a white-and-red spiral.

Identifying marks of the F-3/R 1: inboard air duct, MG 151 guns at the wing joints, wing ETC's.

In 1944 a mixed type, prepared at the front, showed up in great numbers on the eastern front for use as a
192 pursuit bomber. It was based on the Fw 190 A-7 or A-8 basic models, with the outer wing guns removed as
well as the ETC units under the wings. These were used by the III./SG 3 in Courland.

A busy airfield in the central sector, in the summer of 1944. The Hs 129 in the foreground has towing tackle, as good as new, for DFS 230 freight gliders on its tail.

A quick takeoff by a Ju 87 G-2 of the 10.(Pz)/SG 3.

A dive bomber has been made into a (tank) chaser: the type of line marking shows it. The pack commander's plane in the summer of 1944.

No retouching! After taking an anti-aircraft hit in the tail—one steering cable is hanging out—a tank chaser comes in for a landing with its landing gear blown off.

Too big, too slow and too expensive to be a tank chaser: Ju 88 P-3 with two BK 3.7 guns. After brief front testing, the model was called back.

Because of its heavy scattering, the MK 103 did not prove itself as a wing antitank gun. Three Fw 190 F-3/R 3 planes were so equipped by Arado at the end of 1943.

Another cowling variation with better barrel support gave no good results. Only two Fw 190 F-8/R 3's were built by NDW in November of 1944.

The magazine of an Hs 129's MK 103 gun is loaded with hard-core antitank shells with tracers.

An Hs 129 B-3 with the 7.5-cm gun. With this weapon, even the gigantic Stalin tanks could be attacked successfully. Only a few planes got into action with the 14./SG 9 at the beginning of 1945.

On September 30, 1944 Sergeant Otto Ritz of the 10./SG 9 received the Knight's Cross after destroying 70 tanks.

Lower left: After his hundredth mission, Captain Hubert Pölz, Echelon Captain of the 7./SG 3 in the Courland Basin, was awarded the oak leaves on November 25, 1944. The plane is an Fw 190 F-8.

Right: The Echelon Captain of the 10./SG 9, First Lieutenant Weber, still flew an Hs 129 B-2 equipped with the obsolete MK 101.

Major Heinz Frank, Commander of the training unit of the I./SG 152, and First Lieutenant Seyffardt. The instructional crews saw service at the front in Yugoslavia.

General Seidemann with the 10./SG 9; at right is the Echelon Captain, First Lieutenant Weber.

A Fiat CR 42 of NSGr 7 in Croatia at the end of 1944.

Arrangement of the weapon holder for the six recoilless vertical weapons in the fuselage.

The six 77-mm tubes as seen from above.

Experimental equipping of an Hs 129 B-1 with the SG "Förstersonde" device.

The sensor that picks up the electromagnetic field of the tank below projects from the nose. Note the different bow armor, resembling that of the Fw 189 V 1b.

At the end of 1944, new universal drop containers were introduced, capable of holding either 500-liter tanks or 500-kilogram splinter bombs, being dropped as supply containers or, as in the picture below, used to carry personal luggage on a transfer flight.

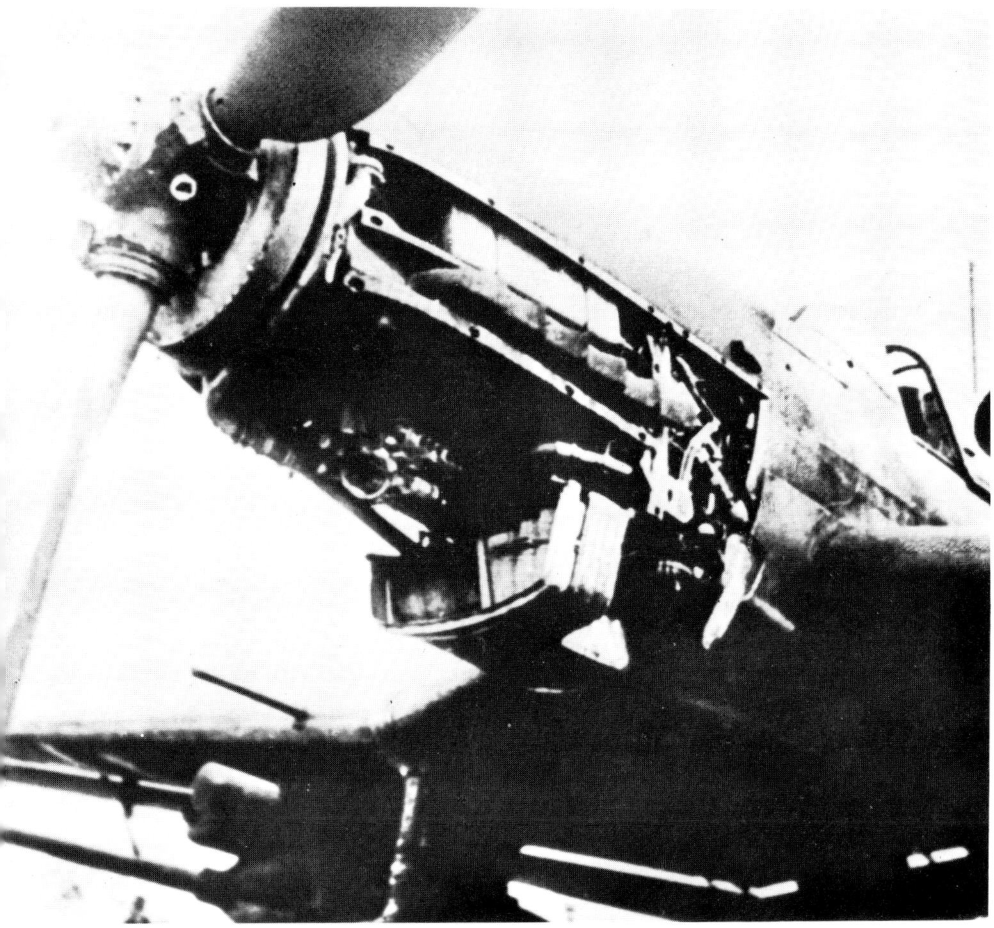

Unusual too: A Ju 87 G-2 with exhaust flame extinguishers, presumably for twilight missions. The yellow band around the fuselage is likewise something unusual.

A Ju 87 D-5 reequipped as a tank chaser, but exceptional in keeping the MG 151 in the wing.

The Fw 190 F-8 was the most versatile German fighter of 1944-1945. The pictures show it with three different bomb loads.

The most frequently used bomb load consisted of a 250-kilogram type on the fuselage ETC and four 50-kg types under the wings.

Four 50-kilogram bombs and a long-range fuel tank were a rare combination.

The F-8/U 1 was more pursuit bomber than fighter plane when it carried a 500-kilogram bomb under the fuselage and a 250-kg bomb on each wing ETC 503.

The WGr 28 mortar shell proved to be unsuitable for use against tanks on account of its slow speed and resulting low probability of hitting its target.

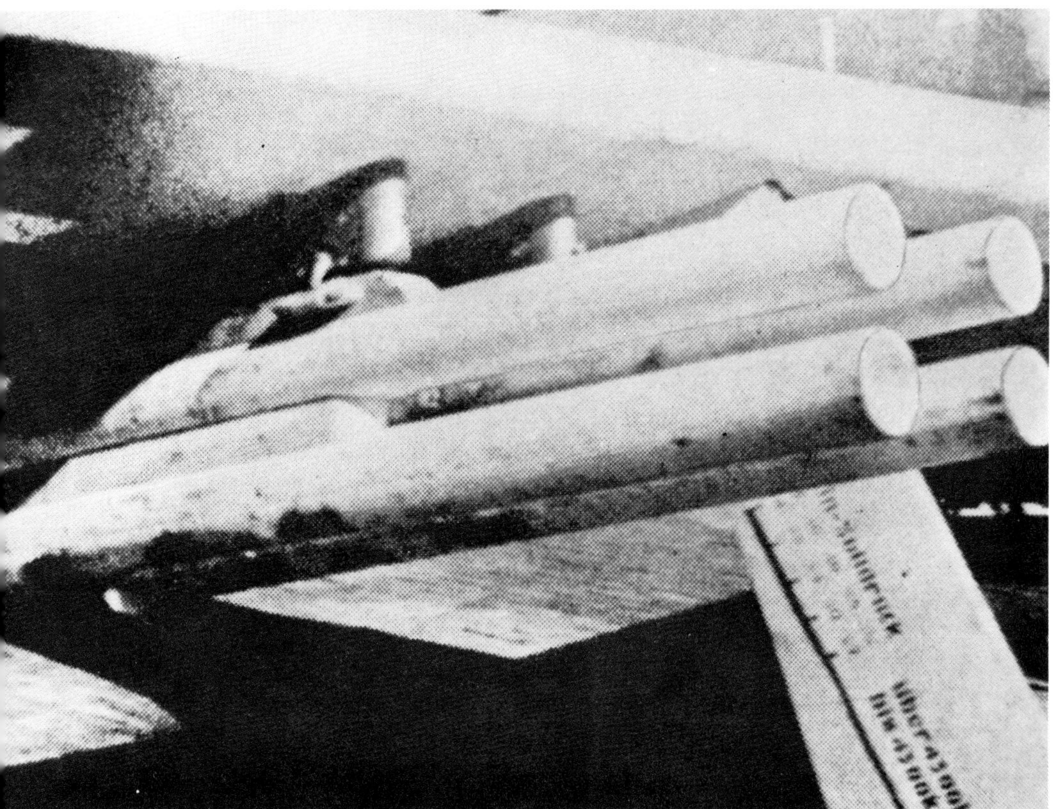

An Fw 190 F-8 with four 8.8-cm "Panzerschreck" rocket-firing tubes. Their range was between 100 and 150 meters.

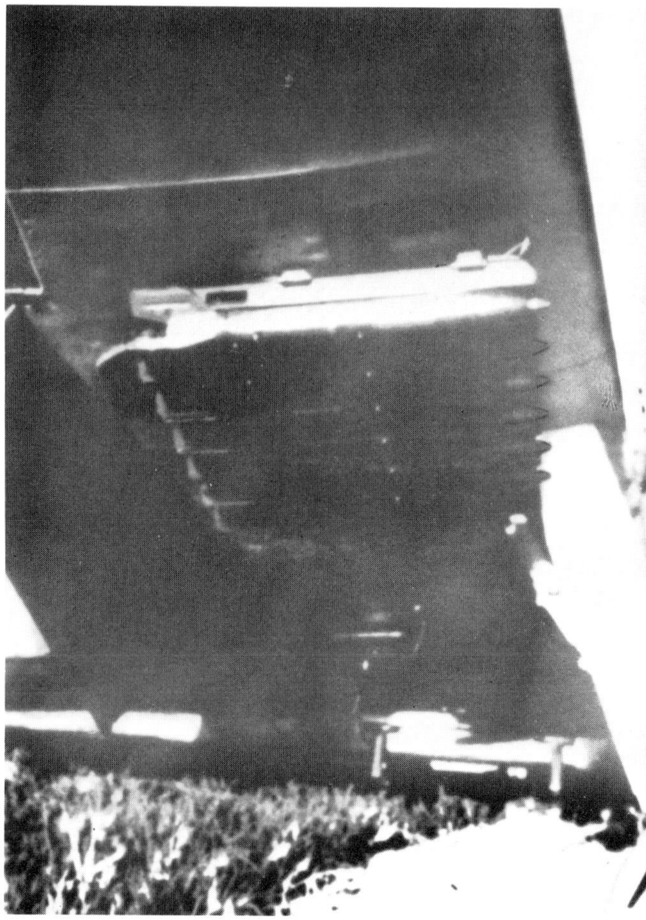

Upper left and below: Experimental installation of two SG 113 "Förstersonde" units in an Fw 190 F-8, factory number 586586. Each device holds three firing tubes. The general disadvantage of the sonde was that, once it was turned on, it registered any large amount of iron. While approaching a tank target, it could just as well fire at a wreck below the plane or a tank on its own side. Upper right: Panzerblitz-1 rockets under the wing of a crash-landed Fw 190 F-8.

Above and center: Fw 109 F-9 planes in perfect winter camouflage. Except for the swastika, all clear lines have been softened by overpainting. II./SG 2 in Hungary, January 1945.

Left: A young pilot of the twilight battle group of the III./KG is congratulated after his 200th mission.

The Siebel Si 204 E light night fighter-bomber was meant to replace the Ju 87 D-8 on the eastern front. It had two fixed MG 151 guns at the wing joints, a rotating turret with an MG 131, and a 500-kg bomb load. A few of these planes saw service with the staff of NSGr 4.

Ju 87 D-8 night fighter planes with the large universal containers.

In May of 1945 many fighter planes were captured in Czechoslovakia.

An Fw 190 F-8/R 1 at the edge of the field at Pardubice, with its weapons removed.

The wreck of an F-8 with "Panzerblitz 1" rockets under its wings.

Fw 190 D-9 and F-9 planes at Milovice; the national emblems were retouched on the photos.

Pursuit and Blitz Bombers, 1942-1945

While what was needed above all in the East was a fighter plane that could carry a maximum bomb load, regardless of the loss in speed caused by having bombs hanging under it, the situation on the Channel coast required a fast pursuit bomber with a long range. In an early developmental stage of the Fw 190, Focke-Wulf had already begun to experiment with pursuit bombers. In June of 1942, Fw 190 A-3/U 1 planes replaced the Bf 109 pursuit bombers in the tenth echelons of JG 2 and 26, which had done outstanding work in holding off the commando operations at Dieppe on August 19, 1942. On the basis of the experience gained there, a beginning was made at the end of 1942 in setting up a four-group SKG 10 as an anti-invasion unit. Naturally this squadron was not to wait idly until a landing took place, but as its name suggests, to carry out surprise attacks on targets in England as a fast battle squadron. Only auxiliary tanks could provide the necessary range. The first pursuit bombers with extended range were the Fw 190 A-4/U 8's, which carried 300-liter tanks on covered Ju 87 carriers under their wings. But since the loss in speed was too great, the A-5/U 8 series was equipped with the so-called Messerschmitt carriers. But since the leadership wanted to be able to hang bombs on the wing carriers when the occasion arose, the A-5/U 13 was built with Focke-Wulf carriers. These series were retroactively renamed G-1, G-2 and G-3 in April of 1943. This model had only an MG 151 in each wing. The G-3 became the standard Jabo-Rei (pursuit bomber with extended range) in the West. The G-8 was dropped from the construction program again in February of 1944, shortly after production had started. Because the Fw 190 had proved itself so well as a pursuit plane, fighter and pursuit bomber, attempts were made to turn it into a "Jato" torpedo carrier. The U 14 and U 17 reequipping sets included enlarged control surfaces and a lengthened tail wheel, plus the complicated aiming apparatus. But the tests were unsatisfactory.

There were versions of the extended-range pursuit bombers for night operations, equipped with exhaust flame dampers.

The success of the SKG 10 was minimal. The available aircraft were in part inferior, and included reequipped Fw 190's of the A-3 to A-5 series. The flying personnel had been gathered from various schools and units and trained "on the double". But a corps spirit was lacking, and the situation was not improved by sending the squadron over England in V or echelon formation.

To defend against a possible invasion, the fighter squadrons in the West, and the night fighters as well, constantly kept a bomb-loaded emergency flight in readiness.

Messerschmitt's frantic attempts to make the Me 210 ready for action at last led to no satisfactory conclusion. In 1942 Test Echelon 210 was formed in Soesterberg; the unit became the 16th echelon of KG 6 in August and flew several missions against England. The successor model Me 410 A-1, on the other hand, was an excellent high-speed bomber highly regarded by the KG 51 pilots. The plane could carry up to two tons of bombs and attain top speeds of around 620 kph; thus it was an opponent that the British night fighters took seriously.

In the 1944 invasion and the resulting fighting on the western front, day and night fighters had to intervene in ground warfare to an increasing degree, though the pilots were hardly trained for it at all. Even unsuitable aircraft models such as the Bf 109 G-6 and G-10, the Fw 190 A-8/R 8 and Fw 190 D-9 assault fighters were used. The highest command was no longer concerned about how many Allied bombers were shot down, but only with how many of their own bomb carriers could take off. Whether they hit their targets was another matter. With this attitude prevailing, even the Me 262 air-superiority fighter was hastened to the front in its A-2 "Blitz Bomber" version. Naturally the "Stormbird" was the fastest pursuit bomber in the world, and its load of two 500-kilogram bombs was a very considerable one, while its armament of two to four 30-mm guns (according to its armament set) was unbelievably strong, but the use of the few planes of KG 51 in this phase of the war had already become senseless. Without a doubt, the Ar 234 B-2 was better suited for use as a high-speed bomber. A bomb load of 1000 kilograms could be carried on bomb locks under each turbine and the chassis, and this could be increased to 1500 kg with takeoff-assistance rockets. The III./EKG 1 and the 1. to III./ KG 76 were equipped with these planes in the autumn of 1944. The KG 76 flew numerous missions against the Remagen bridge in March of 1945, supported by the Me 262's of KG 51.

While only two examples of a further Me 262 bomber type, the A-2/U 2, with glazed nose, were built, a number of further Ar 234 developments were planned, and in some cases also built. The C-3 had an attack armament of two MG 151 guns, the C-8 was to be able to carry 1500-kilogram bombs. In addition, an "army plane" was ordered that, according to RLM concepts, was to be armed with four 5-cm guns. Arado suggested the use of three quadruple launchers for the 21-cm Flak R 42 rockets. These rockets, developed by Krupp, were meant to attain the speed of 580 meters per second, fantastic at that time.

At the beginning of 1945 the German aircraft industry took the attitude that the war could still go on for months, and worked on projects that could have been ready for series production at the end of 1945 at best. Henschel worked on a turbine-powered Hs 132 dive bomber, Junkers on the EF 126, Messerschmitt on the Me 328, powered by two Pulso tubes.

The pursuit-bomber operations of the German pursuit planes, night fighters, pursuit bombers, fighters and night fighters were not used as much against the spearheads of the Allied attack forces, protected as they were by anti-aircraft guns, as against supply networks, depots, troop barracks and airfields. The last great, though costly, attack was made on January 1, 1945, against airfields in Belgium and Holland. As long as fuel supplies lasted, the Luftwaffe continued to attack the enemy in individual missions until the war ended, but most of the time it had to watch impotently while, under the protection of the omnipresent RAF and USAF fighters, hundreds of pursuit bombers smashed their last functioning production and transport facilities as well as their airfields.

Prototypes of the Fw 190 pursuit bomber, works numbers 022 and 023, of the A-0 series.

Fw 190 A-3 planes as pursuit bombers of the IV./SKG 10. The MG FF guns in the wings were removed. The wheel covers were usually removed so that bombs could be hung more easily.

Diagrams of the Fw 190 wing carriers
for Jabo-Rei aircraft.

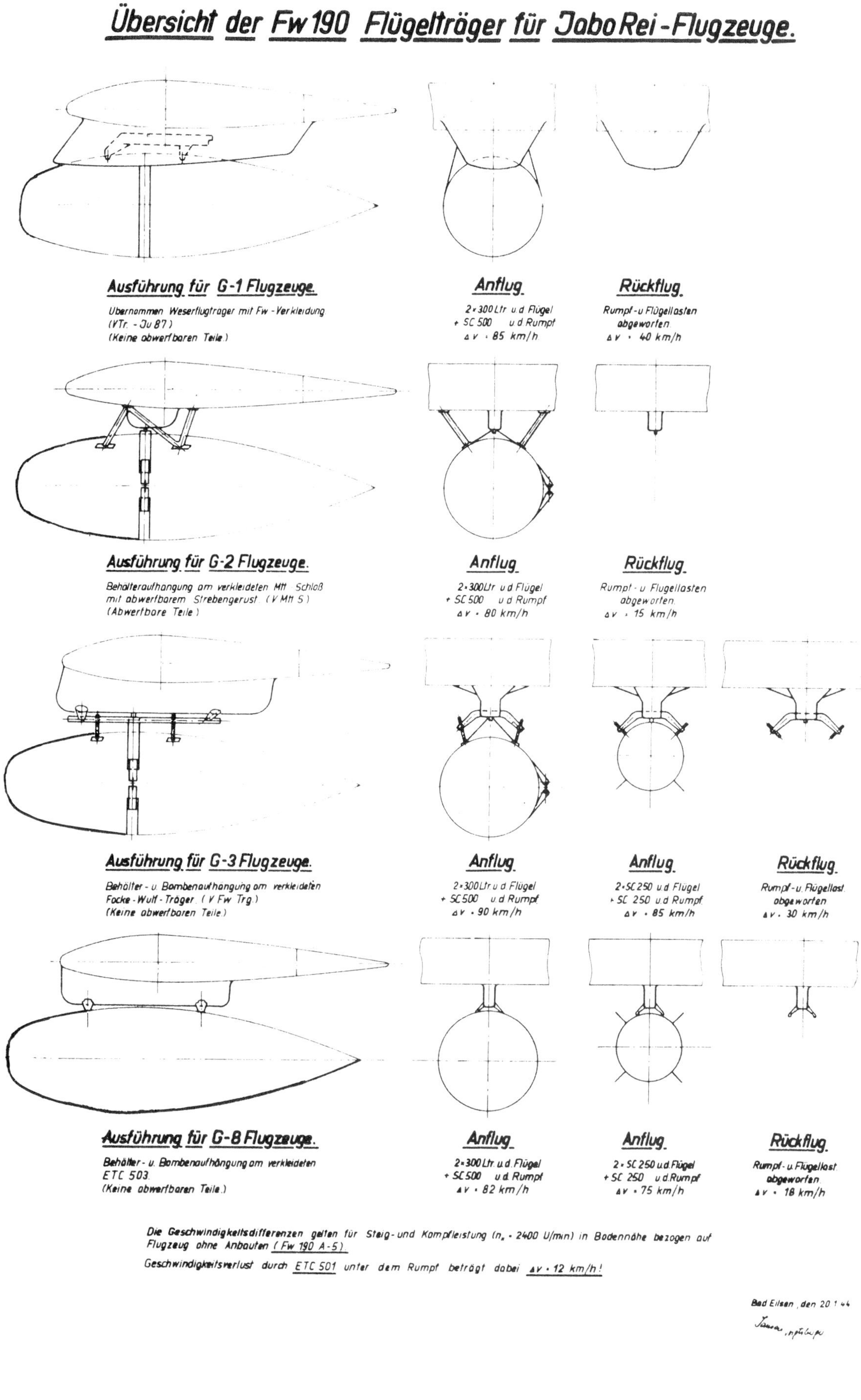

Development of the wing carriers for long-range pursuit bombers of the Fw 190 G-1 to G-3 series.

The Ju 87 carriers on the Fw 190 A-4/U 8 or G-1 were only a temporary solution.

The cowled Messerschmitt carriers on the A-5/U 8 or G-2 gave the least air resistance. On the return flight, the G-2 could attain 640 kph.

The A-5/U 13 could carry either tanks or 250-kilogram bombs on its Fw carriers. As of April 1943 this variant was called the G-3.

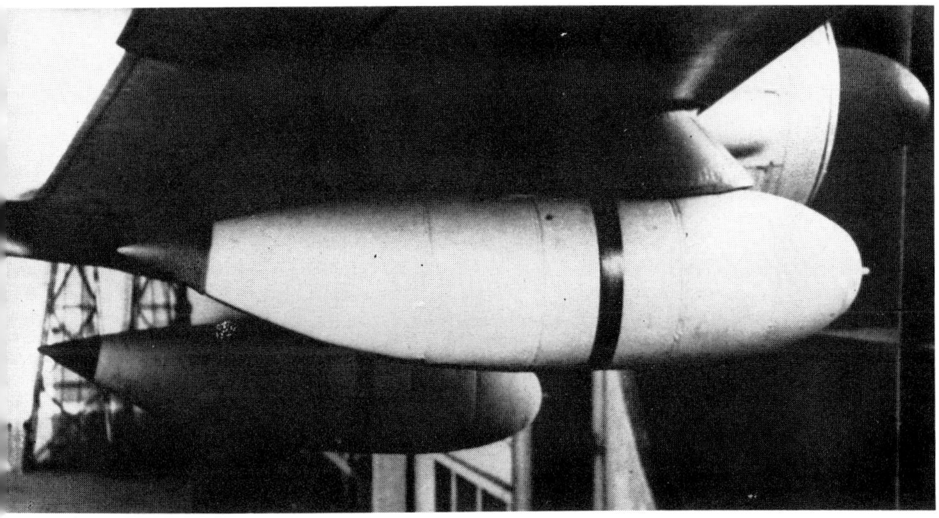

Fw 190 A-5/U 8, the first pursuit bomber with extended range (Jabo Rei) of 1600 kilometers. The MG 17 still mounted in the fuselage was eliminated from the series.

Wind-tunnel testing of the model plane at Chalais-Meudon.

The "normal pursuit plane" reequipped in the field for occasional pursuit-bomber operations retained the moving landing-gear flaps.

Since production of the Fw 190 G-3 began only in April, the SKG 10, when formed in mid-1943, was supplied with reequipped pursuit planes, such as are not found on any type list.

An Fw 190 A-4 without fuselage ETC, but with wing carriers for 250-kilogram bombs.

An Fw 190 A-5 with complete fuselage and wing armament—highly unusual for a pursuit bomber. The antennas of the FuG 16ZY and FuG 25 indicate reequipping in 1944.

A factory-new Fw 190 G-2.

An A-6 pursuit bomber of the III./JG 26, June 1944.

216

A night pursuit bomber Fw 190 G-2/N. The vent aprons over the cooling air exits do not appear to be factory-made. In the port wing: the double spotlight that blinked in Morse code when flying over anti-aircraft emplacements also served as a landing light.

An Fw 190 A-6 pursuit bomber with SB 1000 bomb, its lower fin sawn off.

More effective than the blind cover at the front (see previous page) was this version, which did not go into series production. The bomb in the middle photo is the wooden model of an SB 1000 bomb.

The frontal resistance of the "double rider" tanks on the wings of the plane at right was considerably less than that of the previous tanks on the ETC, but the stability problems could not be overcome.

This auxiliary container was tested by EKdo 25.

An Fw 190 F-8 as the carrier for the remote-controlled BV 246 "Hagelkorn" (hailstone) glider bomb.

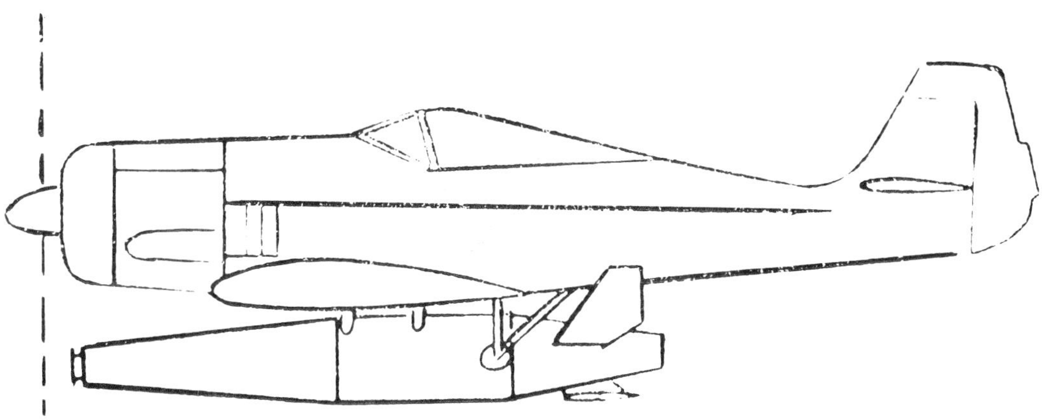

Above and center: Film picture of an Fw 190 with a bomb torpedo under its fuselage. This may be the V 13, a test model with A-3 controls and V motor.

The few Fw 190 F-8 torpedo bombers, known as Jato, were equipped with the FuG precise altimeter.

At Gotenhafen-Hexengrund the Me 410, He 111 and Ju 88, were tested as carriers of the L 10 glider torpedo.

An Me 410 A-1 as a high-speed fighter plane with the I./KG 51: 500-kilogram bomb load, top speed 624 kph. For comparison, the data for the Mosquito BXVi: 1800-kg bomb load, 656 kph.

Compared to the Fw 190, the Bf 109 had the weaker landing gear and the more shot-sensitive motor, and was thus useful as a low-level attack plane to only a limited degree.

Bf 109 pursuit bombers with the 10./JG 26.

An experimental version of the Bf 109 G-0 as an extended-range pursuit bomber. The auxiliary landing gear, which could be dropped, provided the necessary ground clearance when a 500-kilogram bomb was carried.

In 1944 all pursuit squadrons had to intervene in ground warfare more and more often. Their success was minimal, since the pilots had no training for such operations. A Bf 109 G-6 of JG 3.

222 Fw 190 G-2's with new-type exhaust flame dampers, with NSGr 20 in the autumn of 1944.

Major Kurt Dahlmann, Commander of NSGr 20, which came into being through the renaming of the III./KG 51.

Even the assault chasers of the IV./JG 3 had to attack ground targets with their Fw 190 A-8/R 8 planes.

Powerplant test run of an Fw 190 G-2/N of the 3./NSGr 20.

Late in the afternoon the echelon's crews are briefed.

Planes of the 2./NSGr 20, with red lower motor cowlings, are supplied with ammunition. These planes too are not included in any production series: Armament 2 MG 131 and 2 MG 151, like the F-8, but instead of wing ETC's they have Mtt locks for the tanks.

The plane in the lower photo has no flame extinguisher.

Judged by their decorations, only a few of these young pilots of NSGr 20 have had much combat experience.

At sunset the pilots get into their planes and taxi to the runway to take off.

An Fw 190 A-9 as a pursuit bomber, with a fuselage ETC and reduced wing armament, from the 3./JG 11 at Atraussberg, early in 1945.

An extended-range pursuit bomber based on the Fw 190 A-8.

The 3./JG 11 took part in the fighting around Berlin with their Fw 190 A-8 and A-9 planes. The last pursuit planes also had the strengthened armor protection for the pilot and the bowed cabin canopy. Lower left: The small bulges covering the MG 17 mechanisms project from the flat top of the fuselage.

Even high-performance pursuit planes like the Fw 190 D-9 were used as fighters in the last months of the war.

Very unusual: ETC 71's under the wings of a long-nose Fw 190.

The small ETC 504 under an Fw 190 D-9.

Naturally the Me 262 A-2 was considerably faster than any other pursuit bomber, but its massed use as a fighter would have been more sensible. In 1944 the Reich had neither the industrial capacity nor enough personnel to balance the Allied superiority on all fronts with hundreds of jet pursuit bombers.

An Me 262 as a test carrier.

A "Viking ship" bomb carrier with a 500-kilogram bomb.

A maximum bomb load of 1000 kilograms, four 3-mm guns, top speeds of over 700 kph—no other pursuit bomber could show these data in 1945.

The Ar 234 V-9, the first type with retracting landing gear, was tested as a high-speed bomber for 250-kilogram bombs under its motors.

The ETC 503, with its low-resistance cowling, under the turbine of an Ar 234.

An Ar 234 B-2 of the III./KG 76 takes off with rocket assistance.

Maintenance work at the Münster-Handorf airfield.

An Ar 234 B-2 with two 50-kilogram bombs under each motor. As can be seen by the tree in the background, the jet bombers were already in action in the late summer of 1944. There is yellow identifying paint on the turbine air intakes and undersides.

The Ar 234 could not taxi under its own power because of the sensitivity of the powerplants, so it had to be towed to the runway.

Captain Lukesch's Arado being towed by a halftrack cycle. The powerplant intake openings have been covered by caps painted in the echelon color.

The commander's plane is marked by an "A" on the sides of the nose.

The fuselage of the Ar 234 is painted in the new 81/82 colors, plus winter camouflage on the upper surfaces.

Major Baetcher, Commander of the III./KG 76. The letter "A" is painted in green 25, the borders of the handholds in white.

A look inside the full-view canopy of the Ar 234 B-2, showing the RF2C periscope.

When a bad-weather front stopped the Allied pursuit bombers from attacking during the Ardennes offensive, the III./KG 76 at Handorf could afford the time for this inspection.

Fueling an Ar 234 B-2. Under the right wing is the takeoff-assisting rocket.

Left: A maintenance man opens the tank of the Riedel starter. The turbine air intakes were painted the echelon color, here red.
Right: An Ar 234 comes in to land with flaps all the way down.

An Ar 234 is inspected at Karup airfield, Denmark, in May of 1945. The plexiglas panes of the canopy are obviously broken.

The end of the jet Blitz bombers.

A cannibalized wreck of an Ar 234 at Manching.

American troops recover the wreck of an Me 262 A-2/U 2 with glazed nose, out of which the sondes of an acoustic navigation device protrude.

In 1945 the night pursuit planes became night fighters. The Ju 88 G-6 planes of the 7./NJG 5 saw action on the Oder front in April.

In March of 1945, Master Sergeant Migge of the III./NJG 11 flew a Bf 109 G-10, that bore MG 151 guns under the wings, in operations against the bridges at Wesel.

Above: the Do 335 A-1 could carry 500-kilogram bombs in a shaft.

Center: Photo montage of a Ju 288 C with BK 5 guns, which was intended to see action as an armored pursuit plane like the Ju 88 P.

Left: The Bücker Bü 181 of the Bienenstock Command. It was to fire on American tanks in low-level flight with a "mailed fist" under each wing.

The last projects.

The Me 238 was to be a low-cost, mass-produced low-level attack plane with two explosion engines.

A wind tunnel model of the Junkers EF 126 "Ellie". The plane resembled the Fieseler Fi 103 "V-1".

Appendix

Aircraft types

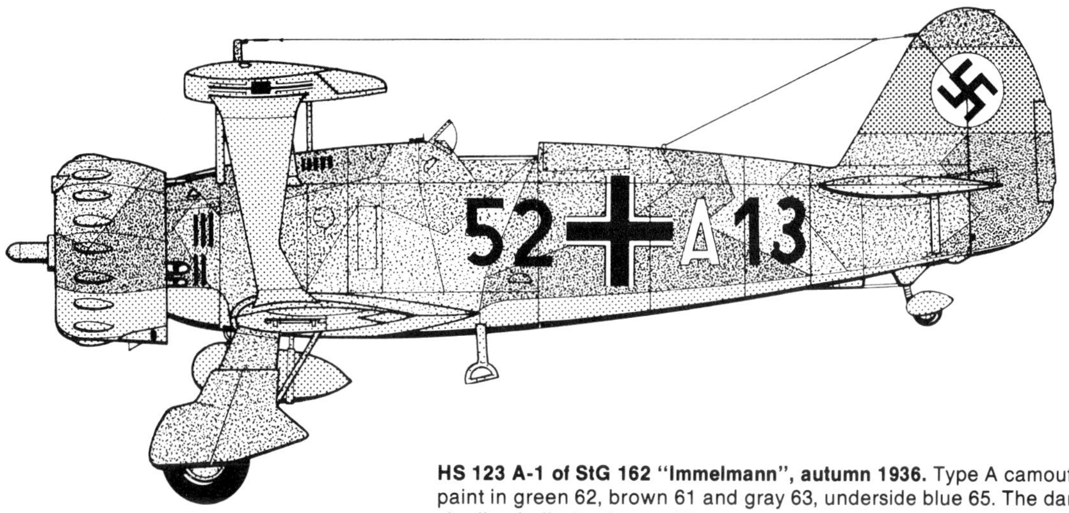

HS 123 A-1 of StG 162 "Immelmann", autumn 1936. Type A camouflage paint in green 62, brown 61 and gray 63, underside blue 65. The darkest shading indicates brown 61.

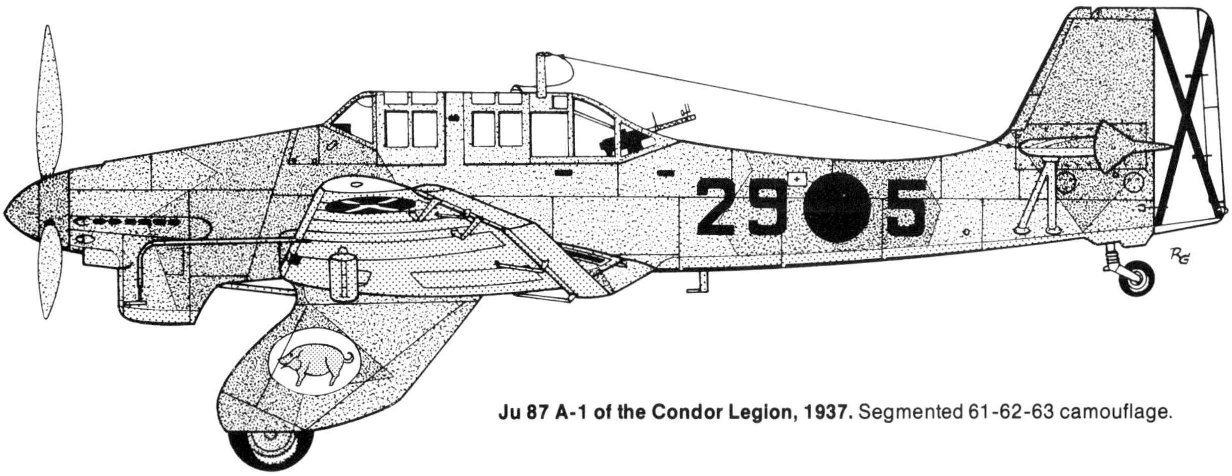

Ju 87 A-1 of the Condor Legion, 1937. Segmented 61-62-63 camouflage.

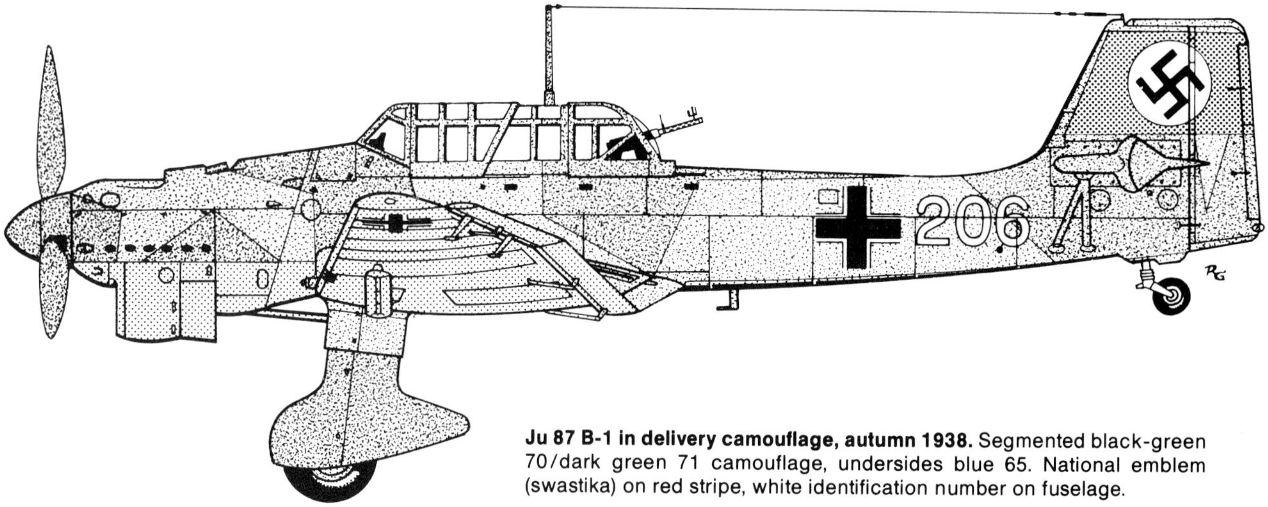

Ju 87 B-1 in delivery camouflage, autumn 1938. Segmented black-green 70/dark green 71 camouflage, undersides blue 65. National emblem (swastika) on red stripe, white identification number on fuselage.

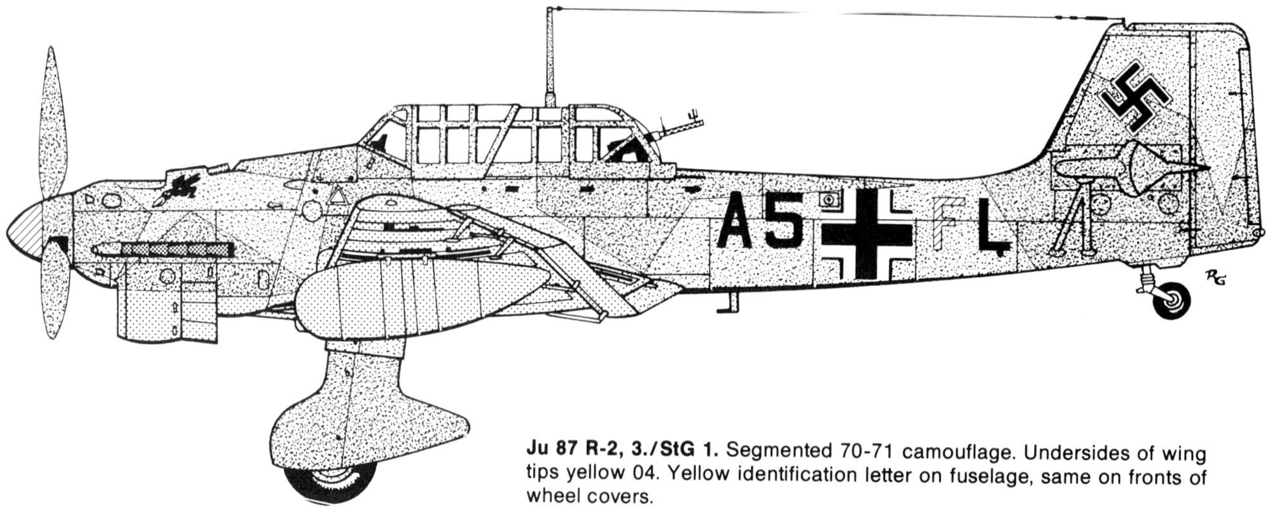

Ju 87 R-2, 3./StG 1. Segmented 70-71 camouflage. Undersides of wing tips yellow 04. Yellow identification letter on fuselage, same on fronts of wheel covers.

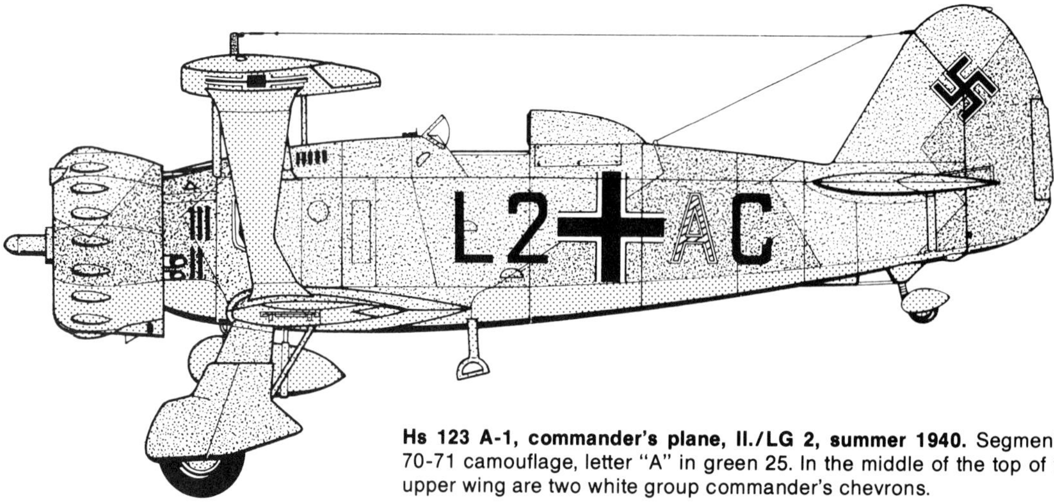

Hs 123 A-1, commander's plane, II./LG 2, summer 1940. Segmented 70-71 camouflage, letter "A" in green 25. In the middle of the top of the upper wing are two white group commander's chevrons.

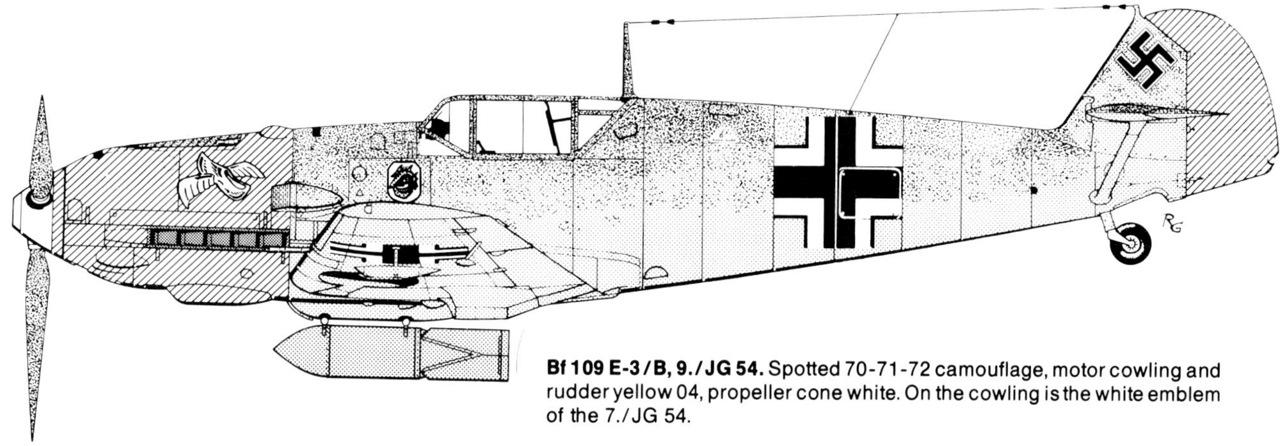

Bf 109 E-3/B, 9./JG 54. Spotted 70-71-72 camouflage, motor cowling and rudder yellow 04, propeller cone white. On the cowling is the white emblem of the 7./JG 54.

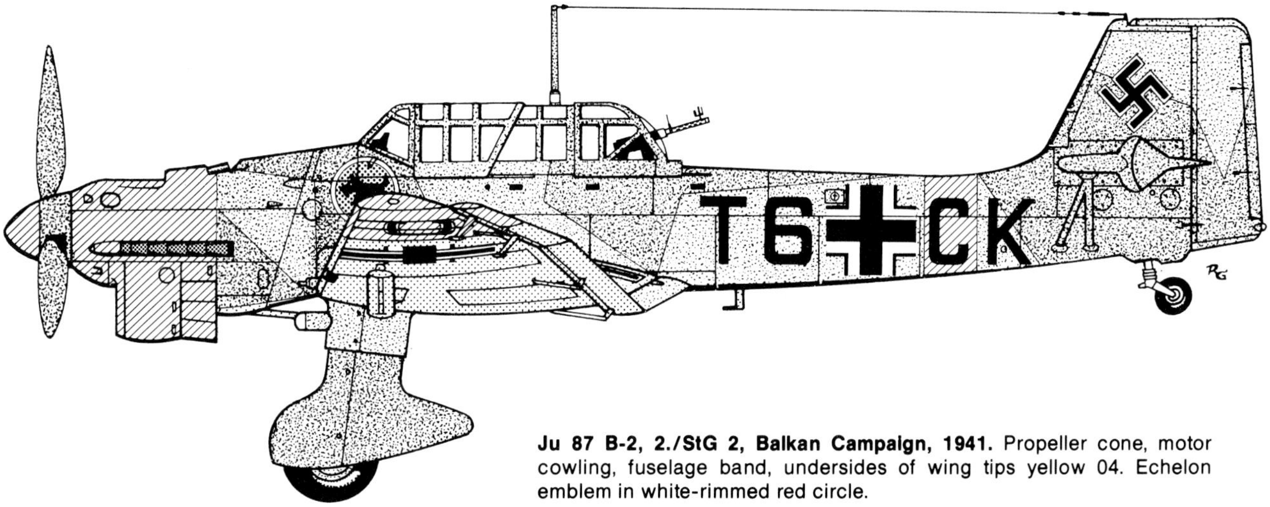

Ju 87 B-2, 2./StG 2, Balkan Campaign, 1941. Propeller cone, motor cowling, fuselage band, undersides of wing tips yellow 04. Echelon emblem in white-rimmed red circle.

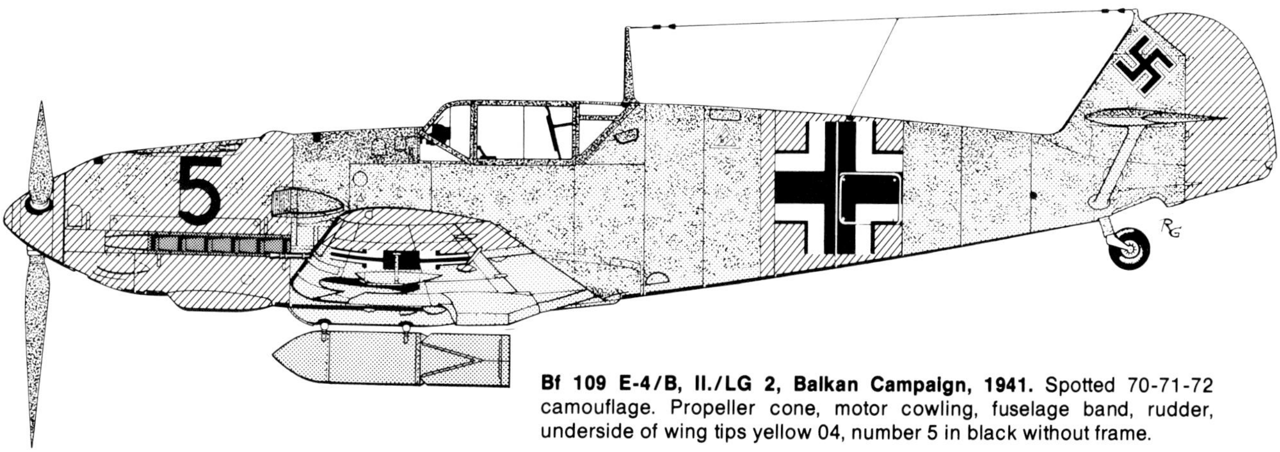

Bf 109 E-4/B, II./LG 2, Balkan Campaign, 1941. Spotted 70-71-72 camouflage. Propeller cone, motor cowling, fuselage band, rudder, underside of wing tips yellow 04, number 5 in black without frame.

242

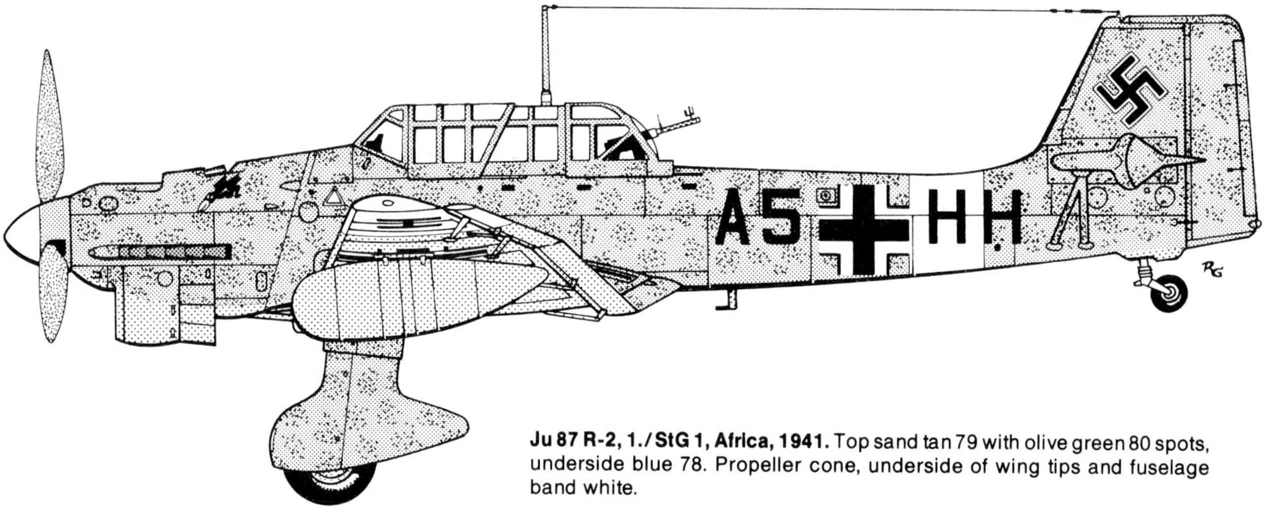

Ju 87 R-2, 1./StG 1, Africa, 1941. Top sand tan 79 with olive green 80 spots, underside blue 78. Propeller cone, underside of wing tips and fuselage band white.

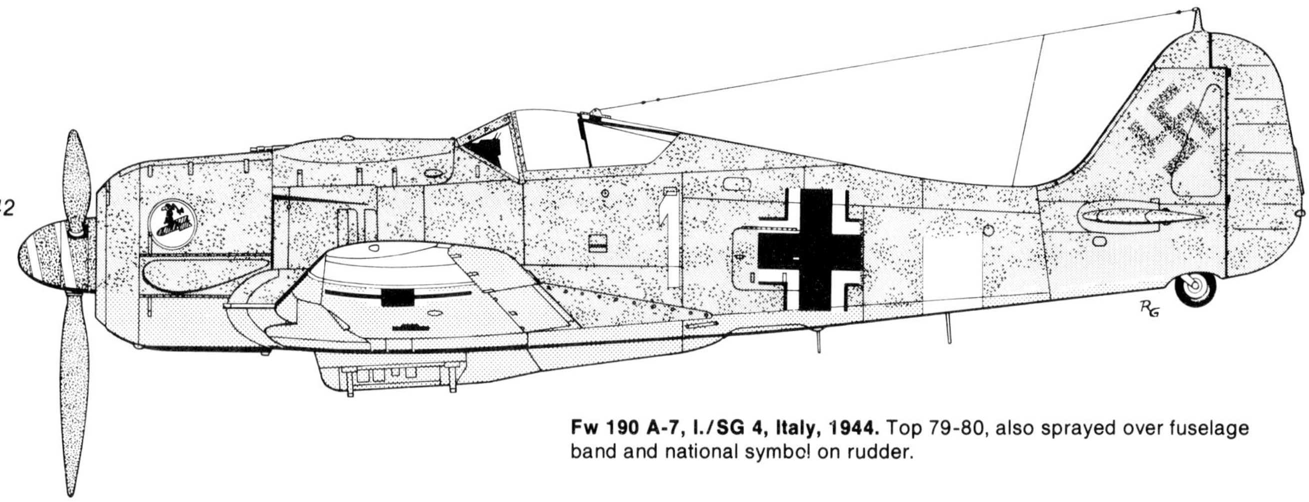

Fw 190 A-7, I./SG 4, Italy, 1944. Top 79-80, also sprayed over fuselage band and national symbol on rudder.

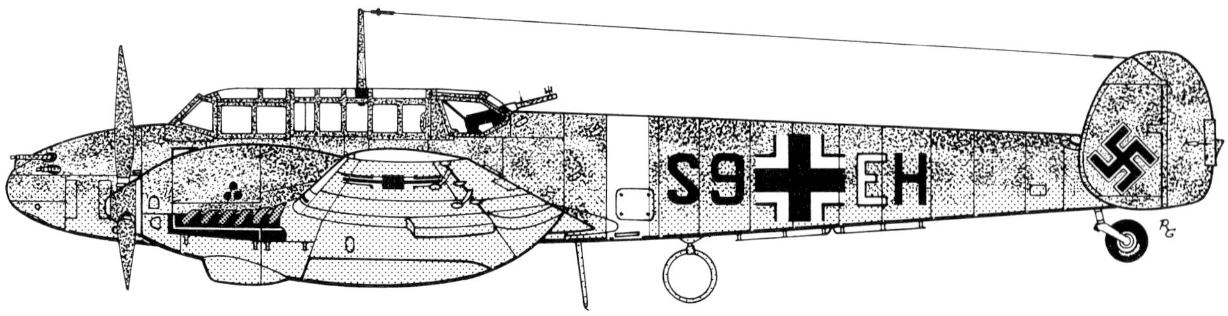

Bf 110 F-0, I./SKG 210, Spring 1942. Spotted 70-71-02 camouflage, fuselage band, leading wing edge and underside of tips white.

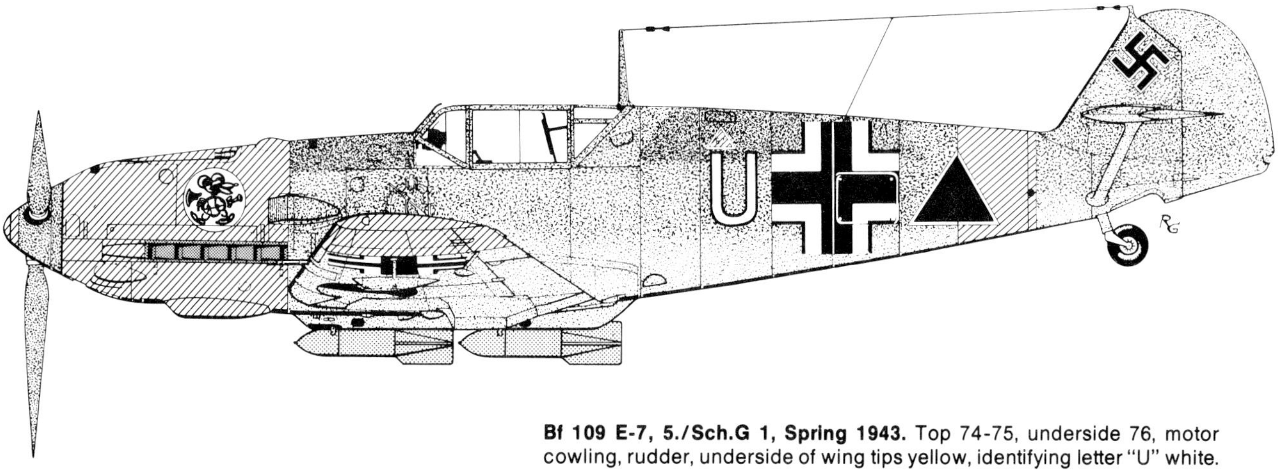

Bf 109 E-7, 5./Sch.G 1, Spring 1943. Top 74-75, underside 76, motor cowling, rudder, underside of wing tips yellow, identifying letter "U" white.

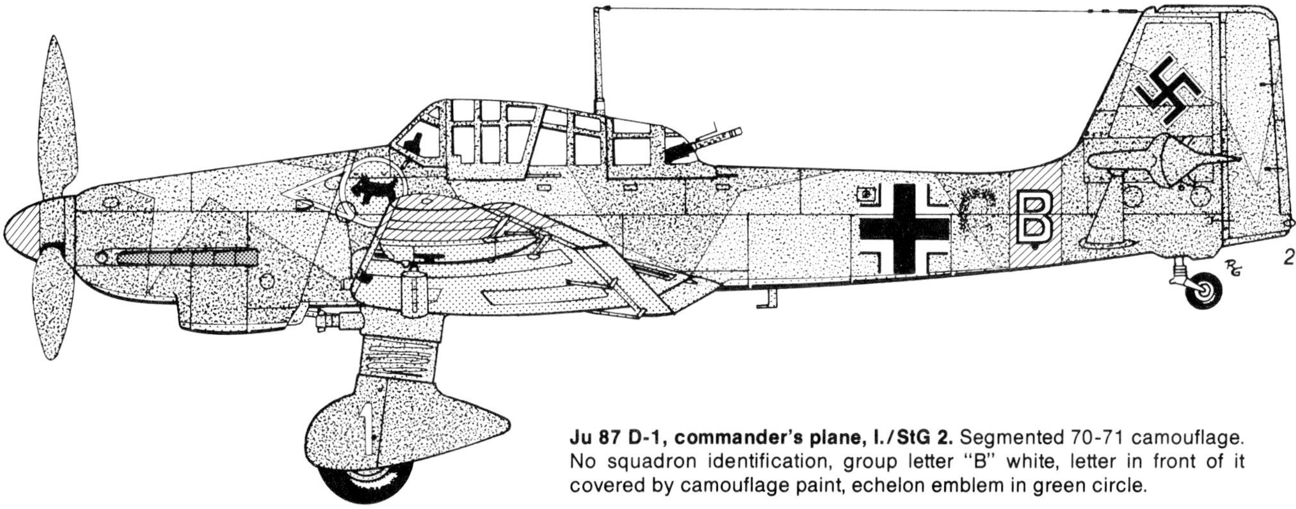

Ju 87 D-1, commander's plane, I./StG 2. Segmented 70-71 camouflage. No squadron identification, group letter "B" white, letter in front of it covered by camouflage paint, echelon emblem in green circle.

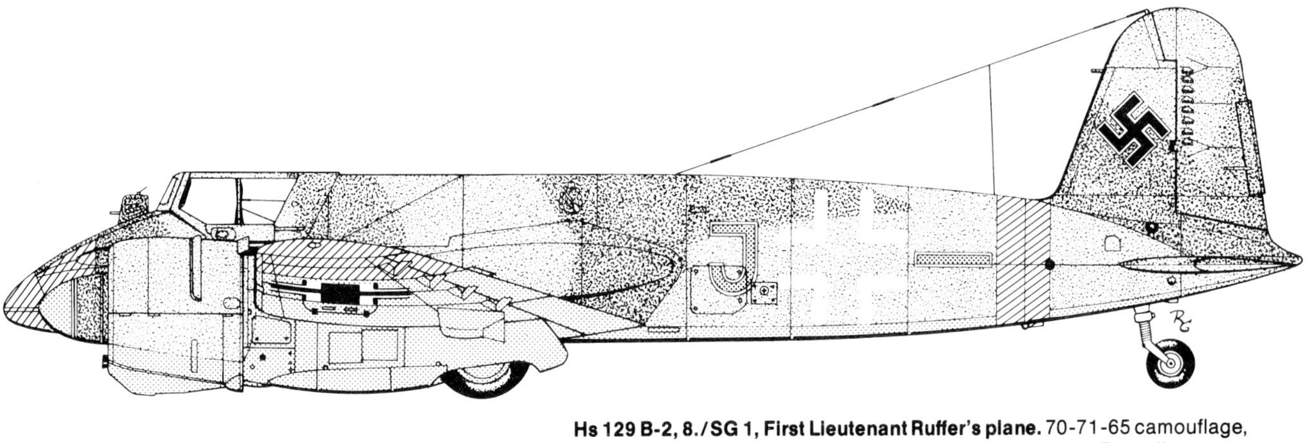

Hs 129 B-2, 8./SG 1, First Lieutenant Ruffer's plane. 70-71-65 camouflage, nose, underside of wing tips, fuselage band yellow. Propeller cone, identifying letter and group bar red.

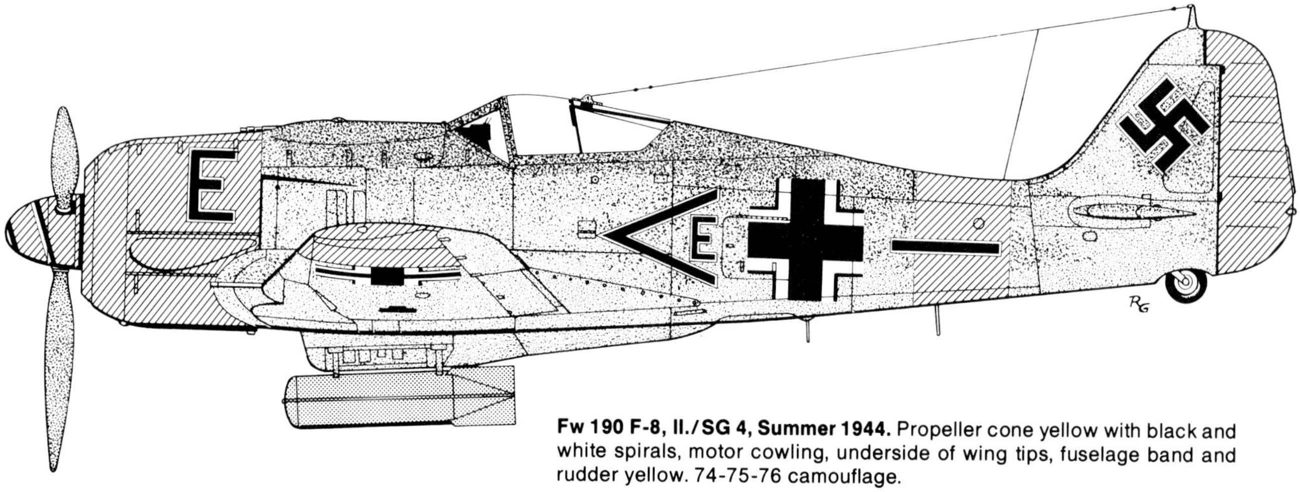

Fw 190 F-8, II./SG 4, Summer 1944. Propeller cone yellow with black and white spirals, motor cowling, underside of wing tips, fuselage band and rudder yellow. 74-75-76 camouflage.

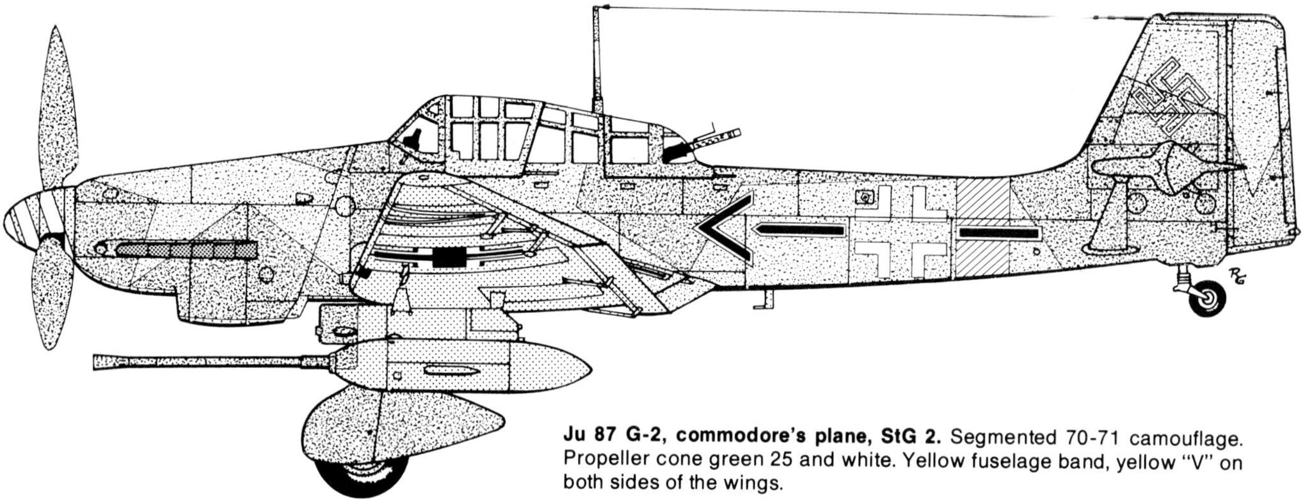

Ju 87 G-2, commodore's plane, StG 2. Segmented 70-71 camouflage. Propeller cone green 25 and white. Yellow fuselage band, yellow "V" on both sides of the wings.

Group and Echelon Emblems

I./StG 2

I./SG 4

I./StG 1

I./SKG 210

9./JG 54

II./Sch.G 1

II.(S)/LG 2